Pacific Flavours

James Lorimer & Company Ltd. acknowledges the support of the Ontario Arts Council for our publishing program. We acknowledge the support of the Government of Canada through the Book Publishing Industry Development Program (BPIDP) for our publishing activities.

This book is dedicated to my loving and supportive family: Mel, Kate, David and Elizabeth Lee.

Cataloguing in Publication Data

Lee, Virginia, 1947-
  Pacific flavours : a guidebook and cookbook

Includes index.
ISBN 0-88780-511-6

1. Cookery – British Columbia. 2. Restaurants – British Columbia – Guidebooks.
I. Title.

TX715.6.L43 2000   641.59711   C00-930894-6

All photos by Hamid Attie, excepting pages 29, 30, 31, 35, 47, 65, 105, 119, 127, 131, 136 (Al Harvey); and pages 85, 109 (Whistler Resort).

James Lorimer & Company Ltd., Publishers
35 Britain Street
Toronto, Ontario
M5A 1R7

Distributed in the United States by:
Seven Hills Book Distributors
1531 Tremont St.
Cincinnati, OH 45214

Printed and bound in Canada.

Pacific Flavours

Guidebook & Cookbook

VIRGINIA LEE
PHOTOGRAPHY BY HAMID ATTIE

James Lorimer Company Ltd., Publishers
Toronto 2000

CONTENTS

SEAFOOD ENTRÉES   *74*

LUNCH, TEA, BREAKFAST *100*

DESSERTS   *116*

PROFILES   *136*

INDEX   *158*

INTRODUCTION

From its southern border shared with the United States to its northern reaches in the subarctic, and from the Rocky Mountains in the east to the vast Pacific Ocean in the west, British Columbia is a magnificent province. Encompassing ninety-five million hectares and with a 7,000-kilometer coastline, it is a land of contrasts diverse yet intrinsically harmonious.

As I travelled throughout British Columbia by air, road and sea to research this book, the sheer raw beauty of the natural environment constantly struck me. On one flight into Vancouver, the sky below was a blanket

of cotton batting penetrated only by jagged mountain peaks. On another flight, the sparkling Pacific Ocean seemed dotted with lush green islands as far as the eye could see. I never tired of driving the roads — the Sea to Sky Highway from North Vancouver to Whistler, the high mountain climb through the Coquihalla Pass, and that unnamed narrow road perched high above the mighty Fraser River in cariboo country. And heading down to the sea on the flotilla of ferries that ply the

coastal waters gave me a greater appreciation of the sometimes serene, sometimes explosive power that the sea lords over the land. The views from all these perspectives are simply spectacular! They have to be seen to be believed.

Along the seafood-rich ocean coastal area, warmed by the Japanese current and protected by a long ridge of mountains, you find the mildest and wettest climate in Canada. In the Fraser River delta, to the south and east of Vancouver, farmers tend a nutrient-rich belt of land that produces a variety of dairy products, meats and produce. Eastward over the Cascade Mountains in the Okanagan Valley, the semi-arid climate, with its hot summer weather and long daylight hours, is an ideal location for fruit farming and wine making. Farther afield to the east, in the Rocky Mountain foothills, large cattle ranches dot the landscape. The abundant variety of quality local foods coupled with a wealth of ethnic products from the province's large international population turns British Columbian kitchens into cooks' playgrounds.

Most British Columbians live in or near Vancouver, Canada's Gateway to the Pacific and third largest city. Spread out from this hub are the less populated but conveniently accessed areas of Victoria and the Islands, the Okanagan Valley and the Whistler resort region. I have chosen to feature these four popular British Columbia destination areas in this cookbook and guidebook.

It was pure enjoyment travelling throughout these areas of British Columbia to research *Pacific Flavours*. I was impressed by and delighted with the quality and expertise of the chefs. The standard of cuisine in Canada's most western province is exceptional, and the recognition it is receiving internationally is truly deserved. I have profiled a sampling of dining establishments that take special interest in promoting cuisine that

uses the best produce and products available in the region. The chefs have different talents, tastes and experiences and were enthusiastic about sharing them with you. You will find that the establishments are quite varied. I trust that this selection will offer something for everyone — from formal gourmet fare to basic home cooking. The common denominator is quality. All restaurants featured in this book are licensed for liquor. Accommodations operated in conjunction with the restaurants are noted and described for easy reference.

Preparing the book for publication was exciting, fun and, at times, challenging. All recipes were tested and

adjusted for your home kitchen in my kitchen, with help from Shari Giffin, an excellent cook and good friend. *Pacific Flavours* is an independent cookbook and guidebook, with no sponsorship or fees paid for inclusion. If you have questions regarding handicap-accessibility or dining and accommodation policies for children please contact the establishment in advance. The accompanying information is up-to-date as of publication, but it is important to keep in mind that restaurant and lodging ownership sometimes changes and that chefs move to other locations.

Following the tradition of the Flavours Series Cookbooks & Guidebooks, I am offering to visitors and residents alike a written and pictorial sampling from many of the best dining establishments found in these regions. Profiles of these establishments can be found at the back of the book. I hope that this journey will inspire you to explore these diverse areas, taking time to sample the wonderful cuisine and wines they offer and, at the same time, drinking in the unbelievable natural beauty. When the excursion is over and you are once again immersed in life's daily routine, pick up this book and rekindle your memories. Picture yourself in the photos and relive that wonderful feeling you had when you were a part of the natural beauty. Prepare and enjoy a delicious meal using recipes from the featured restaurants, and after your satisfying repast, turn to the profiles section to start planning your next trip. Bon appétit!

MAPS

1. The Aerie Resort

2. The Empress Hotel (including)
   Empress Dining Room
   Bengal Lounge
   Kipling's
   Afternoon Tea at the Empress

3. Good Life Bookstore and Café

4. The Grotto

5. Hastings House

6. Herald Street Caffe

7. The Latch Country Inn

8. The Mahle House Restaurant

9. The Old House Restaurant

10. Rain Coast Café

11. Sooke Harbour House

12. Spinnakers Brewpub & Guesthouse

13. The Wesley Street

14. The Wickaninnish Inn & Pointe Restaurant

APPETIZERS

THE PURPOSE OF THE APPETIZER IS TO TEASE ONE'S TASTE-BUDS, STIMULATING THE APPETITE FOR WHAT FOLLOWS... Without a doubt, the chefs who contributed to this chapter have remained true to that intent in these first-course recipes.

Included here are recipes for finger foods such as Tojo's Golden Roll from Tojo's Restaurant. Other recipes, such as Baked Artichokes with Garlic Mayonnaise from Cin Cin, are more suitable for formal sit-down dinners. Some of the recipes are even substantial enough to serve as light dinner or luncheon entrées.

In this section you will sample a wonderful variety of "taste tempters" that showcase the chefs' diverse culinary talents. Rare Ahi Tuna with Asian Papaya Slaw from Whistler's Rim Rock Café highlights delicate Pacific tuna lightly seared to perfection, while Wild B.C. Sockeye Salmon on Red Shiso and Sesame Pancakes from Vancouver's Diva at the Met features paper-thin raw salmon at its succulent best.

Of course no Pacific Northwest cookbook would be worth its salt without recipes including fresh Dungeness crab and Pacific oysters. This celebrated West Coast fare is at its best in Nori-Wrapped Dungeness Crab Cakes with Lemongrass Cream from Oritalia, and in Raincoast Café's Fresh-Shucked Pacific Oysters with West Coast Splash.

I know that you will enjoy trying all of the offerings in this collection and that they will indeed tease your tastebuds.

◀ Grilled Fanny Bay Oysters with Smoked Paprika Mayonnaise

GRILLED FANNY BAY OYSTERS WITH SMOKED PAPRIKA MAYONNAISE

BEACH SIDE CAFÉ, WEST VANCOUVER, BC / *Executive Chef: Carol Chow*

Chef Chow's secret to serving perfect oysters is to make sure that they are not overcooked. Here, she highlights the delicate Fanny Bay oyster with a smoky Mediterranean paprika mayonnaise. Look for smoked sweet paprika in Mediterranean markets. For best results when making the mayonnaise, all the ingredients should be at room temperature.

8	cups water
1	onion, diced
1	leek, thinly sliced
1	lemon, halved
24	preshucked medium to large oysters
1	tbsp vegetable oil
	salt and pepper
	Smoked Paprika Mayonnaise (recipe follows)
	frisée* or other greens for garnish

In large saucepan, bring water, onion, leek and lemon to boil; reduce heat and simmer for 10 minutes. Remove from heat and strain into bowl. Return liquid to saucepan and bring to boil; add oysters, return to boil and immediately remove from heat.

Strain, reserving oyster stock for chowder or fish soup. Cool oysters under cold running water; shake to remove excess water. In bowl, lightly toss oysters with oil, and salt and pepper to taste. Heat grill over high heat; transfer oysters to grill and cook for 30 seconds. Turn and cook for another 30 seconds or until they are just cooked.

TO SERVE: Dollop mayonnaise in centre of each of 4 plates; arrange 6 oysters per plate in spoke-wheel fashion around mayonnaise. Garnish with frisée. *Serves 4.*

* *A member of the chicory family, frisée has curly yellowish leaves.*

Smoked Paprika Mayonnaise

1	egg yolk
2	tbsp white wine vinegar
1	tbsp Dijon mustard
	zest and juice of 1 lemon
1	shallot, minced
1	cup vegetable oil
1	tbsp smoked sweet paprika
dash	Tabasco Sauce
dash	Worcestershire sauce
	salt and pepper

In food processor, purée together egg yolk, vinegar, mustard, lemon zest and juice and shallot. With machine running, very gradually add oil until combined. Add paprika, Tabasco, Worcestershire sauce, and salt and pepper to taste: process for 30 seconds. Taste and adjust seasoning if necessary. Refrigerate until serving. *Makes 1 cup.*

FRESH-SHUCKED PACIFIC OYSTERS WITH WEST COAST SPLASH

RAIN COAST CAFÉ, TOFINO, BC / *Chef de Cuisine: Mark Wrigley*

Like a vintage wine, oysters develop a unique flavour, texture and size depending upon the environment in which they are raised. Of course, native British Columbians claim that the oyster cultivated at Fanny Bay on the eastern coast of Vancouver Island is simply the best. Oyster connoisseurs insist that fresh-shucked oysters on the half-shell are the only way to experience an oyster's true flavour. At Raincoast Café you can partake of that tradition with the café's own special West Coast Splash. Says chef Wrigley, "Splash a spoonful of sauce on freshly shucked oysters, slurp and enjoy."

oysters to serve 4 to 6

West Coast Splash (recipe follows)

Discard any oysters that have damaged shells or that do not close when tapped. Brush with stiff brush under cold running water to remove dirt.

Wrap kitchen towel around your hand to protect it from sharp shell edges. Cup oyster in towel-wrapped hand; with other hand wedge tip of oyster knife into hinge of oyster, twisting until hinge separates. Sever muscle from top shell and remove shell. Gently run knife under oyster just to separate from shell. Set shucked oyster, in its shell, on bed of crushed ice on platter or on individual deep serving plates. Repeat with remaining oysters.

TO SERVE: Present shucked oysters on the shell. Accompany with bowl of West Coast Splash. *Serves 4 to 6.*

1	cup rice wine vinegar
1/3	cup liquid honey
2	tbsp sake (Japanese wine)
2	tbsp minced shallot
1/2	tsp freshly ground black pepper
1/2	tsp red pepper flakes
1/2	tsp salt
1/4	cup minced seeded English cucumber
1/4	cup minced daikon*
1/4	cup minced sweet red pepper
2	tbsp minced green onion
1 1/2	tbsp chopped fresh parsley
2	tsp black sesame seeds

West Coast Splash

In small saucepan over high heat, stir together vinegar, honey, sake, shallot, black pepper, red pepper flakes and salt; bring to boil and immediately remove from heat. Pour into bowl and let cool to room temperature. Cover and refrigerate until thoroughly chilled.

When chilled, stir in cucumber, daikon, red pepper, green onion, parsley and sesame seeds; cover and refrigerate until serving. *Makes 2 cups sauce.*

*Daikon is a large sweet Asian radish available in the produce section of most supermarkets and in Asian markets.

Executive chef's wine suggestion: Pinot Blanc

THAI CURRY BEEF WITH GINGER AÏOLI AND AVOCADO ON HEARTS OF ROMAINE

ORITALIA, VANCOUVER, BC / *Executive Chef: Julian Bond*

Chef Julian Bond has captured true Thai tradition with this appetizer of bold flavours and textures in perfect balance. The curry sauce is sweet and spicy, the aïoli is infused with hot red chili, and the romaine and burnoise of red pepper and cucumber are cold and crunchy. If you are left with extra curry sauce, serve it with grilled chicken or fish. Extra aïoli may be used with fish or cold cooked vegetables.

2	hearts romaine lettuce
1/2	cup finely diced sweet red pepper
1/2	cup finely diced peeled seeded cucumber
1	tsp vegetable oil
1	tsp butter
1	lb tenderloin premium, cut into 1/2-inch cubes
1	cup Curry Sauce (recipe follows)
	Ginger Aïoli (recipe follows)
1	avocado, peeled and diced

Wash romaine hearts and separate leaves; pat dry and set aside. In small bowl, combine red pepper and cucumber to make a burnoise; set aside.

In skillet, heat oil and butter over medium-high heat; briefly sear tenderloin cubes. Add Curry Sauce, stirring to combine. Remove from heat and keep warm.

TO SERVE: Arrange romaine leaves attractively on each of 4 or 6 large chilled plates. Drizzle centre of each leaf with Ginger Aïoli; top with diced avocado and beef. Garnish with burnoise of red pepper and cucumber. *Serves 4 to 6.*

1	tbsp vegetable oil
3/4	cup diced onion
1	tbsp red curry paste*
1	(15 oz/425 ml) can coconut milk
1/3	cup liquid honey
1	tbsp fish sauce*

Curry Sauce

For this recipe, make sure you purchase coconut milk and not cream of coconut which is used mainly for drinks and desserts. When you open the tin of coconut milk, you will find the cream at the top and the watery milk beneath.

In skillet, heat oil over medium heat; sauté onion and curry paste for 4 to 5 minutes or until onion is slightly softened. Add cream from top of coconut milk; cook, stirring often, for about 5 minutes or until mixture splits and caramelizes. Whisk in honey and remaining coconut milk; reduce by half. Stir in fish sauce and reduce slightly. *Makes 1 1/2 cups.*

Look for red curry paste and fish sauce in the specialty section of most supermarkets and in Asian markets.

Ginger Aïoli

1	egg
1	egg yolk
2	tbsp minced gingerroot
1	tbsp minced garlic
1	tbsp sambal oelek*
3/4	cup peanut oil
3	tbsp lemon juice
1	tsp granulated sugar
1	tsp salt

In food processor, combine egg and egg yolk, gingerroot, garlic and sambal oelek; process until blended. With machine running, add half of the peanut oil in thin steady stream. When mixture begins to thicken, add lemon juice, sugar and salt; process until blended. With machine running, add remaining peanut oil, increasing the flow as mixture becomes pale. Cover and refrigerate until serving. *Makes 2 cups.*

Sambal oelek is a curry paste of chilies, brown sugar and salt found in Asian markets.

PAN-SEARED CAMEMBERT WITH SPICY CRANBERRY SAUCE

EDGEWATER LODGE, WHISTLER, BC / *Executive Chef: Thomas Piekarski*

Creamy Camembert literally oozes from its crunchy crust in this hors d'oeuvre, which is delicious spread on bread or crackers. As chef Piekarski does, accompany this appetizer with deep-fried parsley sprigs, assorted crackers, sliced rye bread or baguette and Spicy Cranberry Sauce.

1	egg
2	tsp water
1	wheel Camembert cheese*
1/4	cup all-purpose flour
1	cup bread crumbs
pinch	paprika
	salt and pepper
1/3	cup vegetable oil
1/3	cup butter
	fresh parsley sprigs
	Spicy Cranberry Sauce (recipe follows)

In bowl, beat egg with water. Dust Camembert with flour reserving excess; dip into egg wash, then roll in bread crumbs, pressing to adhere. Sprinkle cheese wheel with paprika, and salt and pepper to taste. (Can be wrapped in plastic wrap and refrigerated for up to 6 hours.)

In skillet or electric frying pan, heat oil and butter to medium-high; fry cheese wheel, turning once, for 5 to 7 minutes or until golden. Carefully remove and drain well on paper towel. Wash parsley, shake dry and dust with flour. Standing back to avoid splatters, drop into hot oil in same skillet. With tongs, quickly remove parsley and drain on paper towels.

TO SERVE: Place cheese wheel on serving plate; garnish with crunchy parsley sprigs. Serve with Spicy Cranberry Sauce. *Serves 4 to 8* depending on size of Camembert wheel.
Cheese wheels come in various sizes, the most common being 4 oz and 8 oz. You may also substitute Brie cheese.

12	oz fresh or frozen cranberries
1 1/4	cups granulated sugar
1	cup water
1/2	cup raisins
1/4	cup diced onion
2	tbsp vinegar
1	tbsp Worcestershire sauce
1/2	tsp salt
1/2	tsp Tabasco Sauce
1	tsp ground cumin

Spicy Cranberry Sauce (supplied by author)

This recipe makes more than required for the above recipe. You may halve the recipe or make the full amount and refrigerate or freeze the extra for another time.

In large glass bowl, combine cranberries, sugar, water, raisins, onion, vinegar, Worcestershire sauce, salt, Tabasco and cumin; microwave at high for 6 minutes. Stir and microwave for 2 minutes longer or until berries pop and sauce begins to thicken. Let cool. Pour into glass jars and refrigerate until serving. (Can be refrigerated for up to 2 weeks or frozen in plastic container for up to 6 months.) *Makes 4 cups.*

Chef's wine suggestion: Pinot Blanc of choice

WILD B.C. SOCKEYE SALMON ON RED SHISO AND SESAME PANCAKES

DIVA AT THE MET, VANCOUVER, BC / *Executive Chef: Michael Noble*

If you have never tried raw fish before and are a little hesitant, then this is the appetizer to confidently begin your experience. The flavours and textures are wonderful and you realize that the thinly sliced fresh salmon is not only good, it is the essence of the dish.

1/2 lb frozen wild sockeye salmon
Red Shiso and Sesame Pancakes (recipe follows)
mizuna greens* to serve 4
Miso Soy Dressing (recipe follows)

Thinly slice frozen salmon as for traditional Japanese sashimi (1/4 inch thick, making all cuts in same direction).

TO SERVE: Divide pancakes between 4 plates; top with mizuna greens. Arrange salmon pieces on top and drizzle Miso Soy Dressing around perimeter of plate. Serve at room temperature. *Serves 4.*

*Mizuna greens are feathery Japanese salad greens found in the specialty produce section of supermarkets. If mizuna is unavailable, substitute mesclun mix.

Red Shiso and Sesame Pancakes

1/2	cup all-purpose flour
1 1/2	tsp granulated sugar
3/4	tsp baking powder
1/4	tsp salt
5	red shiso leaves*, julienned
1	tbsp black sesame seeds
1	egg
1/2	cup milk
2	tbsp butter, melted

In bowl, combine flour, sugar, baking powder and salt; stir in shiso leaves and sesame seeds. Whisk together egg, milk and butter; pour over dry ingredients and stir just until thoroughly moistened. (Do not over mix.)

Heat lightly greased griddle to 375°F and spoon 4 dollar-size portions of batter onto griddle. Cook until bottom is golden and bubbles break on top but do not fill in; flip and cook for 1 minute longer or until lightly browned. *Makes 12 pancakes.*

Shisho leaves are from the perilla plant. Look for them in Japanese markets. If unavailable, substitute fresh basil.

Miso Soy Dressing

1/2	cup grapeseed oil
1/4	cup rice wine vinegar*
1 1/2	tbsp miso paste*
1	tbsp mirin* (Japanese rice wine)
1 1/2	tsp soy sauce
1	tsp sesame oil

In jar with tight-fitting lid, shake together grapeseed oil, vinegar, miso paste, mirin, soy sauce and sesame oil. Taste and adjust seasoning. *Makes 1 cup.*

Rice wine vinegar, mirin and miso paste are available in the specialty section of most supermarkets and in Asian markets.

Chef's wine suggestion: Hester Creek Grand Reserve or Okanagan Valley Pinot Blanc VQA 1996.

NORI-WRAPPED DUNGENESS CRAB CAKES WITH LEMONGRASS CREAM

ORITALIA, VANCOUVER, BC / *Executive Chef: Julian Bond*

Sweet fresh Pacific Dungeness crab blends well with the slightly salty strips of sushi nori that wrap these delectable crab cakes. Add to this the unique lemon-ginger flavour of chef Julian Bond's Lemongrass Cream sauce and you have an appetizer or luncheon dish that will leave guests in awe. Garnish servings as desired with fresh herbs, edible flowers or enoki mushrooms.

1	lb Dungeness crabmeat
3	green onions, chopped
1	clove garlic, crushed
4	tbsp Habañero Mayonnaise (recipe follows)
1	tbsp granulated sugar
1	tbsp lime juice
1	tsp coarsely ground pepper
1	egg, lightly beaten (optional to moisten)
3	sheets sushi nori*
	egg wash (1 beaten egg + 1/2 tsp water)
1/2	cup all-purpose flour
2	cups bread crumbs
	vegetable oil
	Lemongrass Cream (recipe follows)

Clean and check crab for shell and cartilage: squeeze to remove excess liquid. In bowl, combine crab, green onions, garlic, Habañero Mayonnaise, sugar, lime juice, pepper, and enough egg to moisten (if desired). Using about 3 tbsp mixture per crab cake, form into circles. Cut sushi nori strips to width of circles and attach, moistening ends with some of the egg wash to seal. Coat open sides of circles with flour; dip in remaining egg wash, then bread crumbs.

In skillet, heat 1/2 inch oil over medium-high heat; fry crab cakes, turning once, for 5 to 7 minutes or until cooked through and light golden. Remove with slotted spatula and drain on paper towels.

TO SERVE: Creatively arrange crab cakes and Lemongrass Cream on individual dishes with garnish of choice. *Serves 4 to 6.*

*Sheets of dried seaweed are available in the specialty section of some supermarkets and in Asian markets.

1	egg
1/4	cup olive oil
1	tbsp lime juice
1	tbsp finely diced seeded Habañero chili pepper
1/4	cup vegetable oil
	salt

Habañero Mayonnaise

Use this hot mayonnaise as a dressing for sandwiches or as a dipping sauce. It can be refrigerated for up to 4 days. Remember not to touch your eyes when handling Habañero chilies as they will burn. Wash hands after dicing. All ingredients should be at room temperature before combining.

In food processor, beat egg; with machine running, slowly add olive oil in thin steady stream. When mixture begins to thicken, blend in lime juice and Habañero chili pepper. With machine running, slowly add vegetable oil, increasing the flow as mayonnaise thickens and pales. Season with salt to taste. *Makes 3/4 cup.*

Lemongrass Cream

1	tsp vegetable oil
1/4	onion, diced
1/4	sweet yellow pepper, diced
1	clove garlic, minced
1/3	cup white wine
3	tbsp lemon juice
1	stalk lemongrass, cut in 2-inch lengths and crushed
1/4	cup crushed gingerroot
1	cup 35% cream
1/2	cup cooked mashed potato
1	tbsp liquid honey
	salt and white pepper

In saucepan, heat oil over medium-low heat; sweat onion, yellow pepper and garlic until vegetables are softened. Increase heat to medium; deglaze pan with wine and lemon juice. Enclose lemongrass and ginger in cheesecloth bag; add to sauce along with cream and potato. Reduce by half.

Remove cheesecloth bag, squeezing to extract juices. Add honey to sauce, season with salt and pepper to taste. In food processor, purée sauce; strain through fine-mesh sieve. *Makes 1 cup.*

RARE AHI TUNA WITH ASIAN PAPAYA SLAW

RIM ROCK CAFÉ, WHISTLER, BC/ *Owner/Chef: Rolf Gunther*

The influence of other Pacific Rim countries is evident in Rolf Gunther's exquisitely prepared seared tuna on a fresh-tasting tropical papaya slaw.

1/2	lb Ahi tuna
1	tbsp extra-virgin olive oil
	salt and pepper
	cayenne pepper
1	ripe papaya, peeled and sliced
1/4	head sui choy, thinly sliced (or
1/4	head bok choy)
1	small red onion, thinly sliced
1	carrot, sliced into ribbons
	Lime Sesame Dressing (recipe follows)

Brush tuna with olive oil; season with salt, pepper and cayenne pepper to taste. Heat heavy-based skillet over high heat; sear tuna for 3 to 4 minutes per side or until rare.

In bowl, toss together papaya, sui choy, onion, carrot and enough of the dressing just to coat.

TO SERVE: Spoon slaw onto plates. Slice tuna very thinly and arrange decoratively over slaw. *Serves 4.*

1/4	cup soy sauce
1/4	cup mirin (Japanese rice wine)
2	tbsp lime juice
1 1/2	tsp minced gingerroot
1	green onion, sliced
1	tsp chopped fresh coriander
1	clove garlic, minced
1	tsp toasted sesame seeds*
1/2	tsp red pepper flakes
2	tbsp peanut oil
1	tsp sesame oil

Lime Sesame Dressing

In bowl combine soy sauce, mirin, lime juice, gingerroot, onion, coriander, garlic, sesame seeds and red pepper flakes; stir until combined. Gradually add peanut and sesame oils, whisking briskly until dressing is smooth. *Makes 3/4 cup.*

*To toast sesame seeds, heat skillet over low heat; cook sesame seeds, stirring constantly for 2 minutes or until golden.

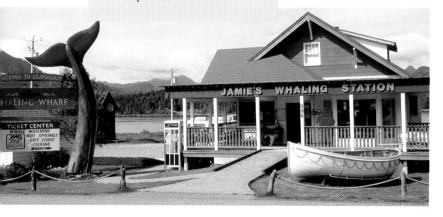

BAKED ARTICHOKES WITH GARLIC MAYONNAISE

CIN CIN, VANCOUVER, BC / *Executive Chef: Romy Prasad*

When selecting artichokes choose ones that are heavy, with tightly closed leaves. Open leaves indicate that the flower bud is overripe.

4 to 6	large globe artichokes
	juice of 1 lemon
	water
8	tbsp + 1/4 tsp extra-virgin olive oil
1 3/4	cup thinly sliced onions
1 1/2	cup diced sweet red pepper
1 1/2	cup diced sweet green pepper
1 1/2	tbsp red wine vinegar
1	tbsp chopped fresh thyme (or 1 tsp dried)
2	bay leaves
2	cloves garlic, minced
	salt and pepper
1	cup soft bread crumbs
2	tbsp chopped fresh parsley
1/2	cup dry white wine
18 to 24	Kalamata olives
	Garlic Mayonnaise (recipe follows)

With a sharp knife remove outer leaves from artichokes. Break off stems and slice across bottoms to create a flat base. Grasp artichoke tops and cut off top two-thirds; discard tops. Holding artichoke bottoms in palm of hand, pull out central cone and remove the hairy choke.

Place artichokes in bowl and combine lemon juice with enough water to cover artichokes. This will prevent discolouration.

In skillet, heat 4 tbsp. of olive oil; add 1 cup onion, red and green peppers, vinegar, thyme, bay, garlic, salt and pepper. Sauté over medium heat until vegetables are softened, about 6 minutes; remove to 9" x 13" baking pan and reserve.

In same skillet, add 4 tbsp. olive oil, and 3/4 cup onion; sweat onion over medium-low heat until soft, about 6 to 8 minutes. Add breadcrumbs and parsley; stir to combine.

Dry artichokes and sprinkle with olive oil, salt and pepper to taste. Fill artichokes with bread crumb mixture; place upright on vegetable mixture in 9" x 13" oblong baking pan. Pour wine around artichokes. Cover with foil, sealing edges. Bake in 350oF oven for 1 1/4 hours.

TO SERVE: Place artichokes on each of 4 or 6 plates; spoon some of the vegetable mixture around artichokes. Pass olives and Garlic Mayonnaise alongside. *Serves 4 to 6.*

2	egg yolks
3	cloves garlic, crushed to paste
1	cup vegetable oil
1 1/2	tbsp warm water
1	tbsp white wine vinegar
3	tbsp extra-virgin olive oil

Garlic Mayonnaise

In food processor, process egg yolks and garlic until combined. With machine running, slowly add vegetable oil in thin steady stream. When mixture begins to thicken add water and vinegar; process until blended. With machine running, add olive oil and process until thickened. *Makes 1 1/2 cups.*

TOJO'S GOLDEN ROLL

TOJO'S RESTAURANT, VANCOUVER, BC / *Restaurateur: Hidekazu Tojo*

British Columbian's of all ethnic backgrounds love the Asian influence in their cuisine, and sushi is a popular item with most residents. Sushi bars serving traditional first-course sashimi followed by a variety of sushi abound in Metro Vancouver. This special "golden roll" of sushi rice, fresh seafood and daikon sprouts is enclosed in a delicate thin egg crepe for excellent presentation and wonderful taste.

4	egg crepes (recipe follows)
	sushi rice (recipe follows)
1 1/2	tsp wasabi paste (Japanese horseradish)
2	tbsp mayonnaise
6	prawns, peeled, deveined and halved lengthwise
1/4	lb salmon, chopped
1/4	lb fresh crabmeat
1/4	lb scallops, chopped
1 1/2	cups daikon sprouts (or other fine sprouts of choice)
	flying fish roe (or fish roe of choice)
	gari (pickled ginger)

Place bamboo mat on work surface with long edge facing you. Place crepe golden side down on closest long edge of mat. Pat one-quarter of the rice over bottom half of the crepe leaving a half-inch space on the side and bottom edges. Spread thin band of wasabi across centre of rice. Arrange one-quarter of the prawns, salmon, crabmeat, scallops and daikon sprouts parallel to the wasabi. Spread thin band of mayonnaise parallel to the seafood.

Lift up the end of mat closest to you and using the mat as a guide, roll the crepe up firmly from the bottom, enclosing the crepe around the rice and seafood. Roll off the mat onto a cutting board and with a sharp knife cut roll crosswise into six equal pieces. Repeat with remaining crepes and filling.

TO SERVE: arrange sliced rolls on individual serving plates. Spoon flying fish roe on each slice and garnish with gari. *Serves 4 to 6.*

*Bamboo rolling mats are sold in Japanese specialty stores. If you can't find one, a folded tea towel is a good substitute.

3	eggs
	vegetable cooking spray

Egg Crepes

At Tojo's Restaurant the cooks make these crepes in a rectangular tamago-yaki pan. If you do not have one, increase the eggs to 4 and cook the crepes in an electric frypan. Cut the cooked crepes into 8 x 7 inch rectangles.

In bowl beat eggs lightly. Spray thin film of vegetable oil into pan. Heat tamago-yaki pan to medium or turn electric frypan to 300°F. Pour 1/4 of the beaten egg into pan and spread to form a thin crepe. Cook for one minute until light golden. Gently lift crepe from pan with spatula and lay on waxed paper to cool. Repeat with remaining egg. *Makes 4 crepes.*

Sushi Rice

1/4	cup rice vinegar
1	tbsp sugar
1/2	tsp salt
1	inch square piece of kelp
1 1/2	cups Japanese short-grain rice
2	cups cold water

In bowl, stir together vinegar, sugar and salt until sugar is dissolved. Add kelp; cover and refrigerate for at least 2 hours or for up to 12 hours.

Rinse rice until water runs clear. In saucepan, combine rice and water; bring to boil. Cover and reduce heat to very low; simmer for 15 minutes or until liquid is absorbed. Remove from heat and let stand 10 minutes. Transfer rice to shallow dish.

Remove kelp from vinegar mixture, discarding kelp. Pour liquid over warm rice and mix well. Let cool until no longer steaming. Cover with damp towel and cool until using. *Makes 4 cups.*

S O U P S

SOUPS ARE PERHAPS THE MOST VERSATILE AND SATISFYING RECIPES IN A COOK'S REPERTOIRE.

When collecting these recipes I asked the chefs to share soups that are representative of their establishment and locale. As a result, they took full advantage of local seasonal produce and seafood. Their contributions are exceptional and feature a variety of ingredients, cuisines and cooking styles.

Chef Patt Dyck from The Country Squire offers us her Leek and Fennel Soup and Sweet Red Pepper Soup — both of which highlight fresh local produce. As an added bonus she shares her recipe for Double-Strength Chicken Stock to ensure the richest soup possible.

On a warm summer day, serve chilled Sweet Pea Soup with Crème Fraîche and Hand-Peeled Shrimp from North Vancouver's Beach Side Café or Vichyssoise with Lobster Medallions from Le Crocodile. When autumn rains begin to freeze into the snowflakes of winter, warm your soul with Maureen Loucks' rich Smoked Gouda Soup from The Mahle House Restaurant or Raincoast Café's Indonesian Sweet Potato, Coconut and Peanut Soup.

The influence the Pacific Ocean has on British Columbia cuisine is evident in the abundance of delicious soups and chowders featuring seafood. For special occasions, start the menu with elegant Pacific Oyster Stew from the kitchen of Pierre Delacote at Seasons Restaurant in Queen Elizabeth Park or the subtle Lobster Bisque from The Empress Room at The Empress hotel in Victoria.

◀ Leek and Fennel Soup

LOBSTER BISQUE

THE EMPRESS ROOM AT THE EMPRESS HOTEL, VICTORIA, BC / *Executive Chef: David Hammonds*

Smooth and subtle best describes this delicious traditional bisque from the elegant Empress Room. Lobster bisque is an excellent secondary dish from a meal of fresh lobster. Simply save the shells for lobster stock and a small portion of the meat for garnish.

3	tbsp butter
1	stalk celery, sliced
1	carrot, sliced
1	large leek, chopped
1	onion, chopped
2	tbsp all-purpose flour
4 1/2	cups Lobster Stock (recipe follows)
1 1/4	cups 35% cream
	pinch cayenne pepper
	salt
1/2	cup lobster meat, cut in chunks

In heavy-based saucepan melt butter over medium heat; sauté celery, carrot, leek and onion, stirring gently, for 5 minutes. Whisk in flour and cook for 1 minute, stirring constantly. Whisk in stock until smooth; cook for about 20 minutes or until vegetables are tender.

In blender or food processor, purée soup in batches. Return to saucepan over medium heat; stir in cream, cayenne pepper and salt to taste. Stir in lobster meat. Garnish with fresh herbs or edible flower petals. Ladle into bowls. *Serves 4.*

	shells from 2 or 3 lobsters
6	cups water

Lobster Stock

You can cook the stock in advance and freeze for later use.

Crack or break up lobster shells into small pieces, being careful not to pulverize.

In large saucepan, combine lobster shells and water; bring to boil. Reduce heat to medium-low and simmer until reduced to 4 1/2 cups. Strain through fine-mesh sieve to remove all traces of shell. *Makes 4 1/2 cups.*

LEEK AND FENNEL SOUP

THE COUNTRY SQUIRE, NARAMATA, BC / *Owner/Chef: Patt Dyck*

The soups at The Country Squire have a special rich flavour because they contain chef Patt Dyck's own Double-Strength Chicken Stock. If you do not have the time or inclination to make stock, you may substitute any good-quality store-bought chicken stock, but be prepared to lose a little of the robust flavour.

3	tbsp olive oil
2	tbsp butter
2	medium leeks (white part only), chopped
2	fennel bulbs, trimmed and chopped
1/4	tsp salt
5	cups Double-Strength Chicken Stock
1	bouquet garni (parsley, bay leaf, thyme and rosemary tied in cheesecloth bag)
1/2	cup 35% cream
	salt and white pepper

In large, heavy-based saucepan, heat oil and butter over medium low heat; add leeks and fennel, stir well and sprinkle with salt. Cover and cook over low heat, stirring occasionally and being careful not to burn, for about 10 minutes or until softened.

Add chicken stock and bouquet garni; simmer, covered, for 30 minutes. Remove bouquet garni. In food processor, purée soup in batches. Strain and return to saucepan over low heat; pour in cream and simmer, stirring, until heated through. Season with salt and pepper to taste. Ladle into bowls. *Serves 4.*

DOUBLE-STRENGTH CHICKEN STOCK

THE COUNTRY SQUIRE, NARAMATA, BC / *Owner/Chef: Patt Dyck*

This recipe has two lists of ingredients as there is a second stage with a slight variation. If you take the time and effort to prepare this rich stock, you will be doubly pleased with the results of your soup.

Ingredients for Stage 1:

4	lb fresh chicken bones
20	cups cold water
2	stalks celery, sliced
2	carrots, sliced
1	onion, chopped
1	bouquet garni (parsley, thyme and bay leaves tied in cheesecloth bag)
1	tsp black peppercorns

Ingredients for Stage 2:

4	lb fresh chicken bones
10	cups cold water
10	cups chicken stock (from Stage 1)
2	stalks celery, sliced
2	carrots, sliced
1	onion, chopped
1	bouquet garni (see Stage 1)
1	tsp black peppercorns

Stage 1:

In stockpot cover bones with water; bring to boil. Reduce heat to low and simmer for 15 minutes, skimming off foam as it rises to surface until top is almost clear.

Stir in celery, carrots, onion, bouquet garni and peppercorns; reduce heat to low and simmer, without stirring, for 3 to 4 hours until liquid is reduced by half. Strain stock into large pot; refrigerate, uncovered, for 4 to 6 hours or until cold and fat is congealed on surfaces. Skim off and discard surface fat.

Stage 2:

Repeat method for Stage 1, using fresh bones and other ingredients listed for Stage 2. Strain double stock. Refrigerate, uncovered, for 4 to 6 hours or until fat is congealed on surface. Skim off fat and freeze in airtight container. Let thaw before using. *Makes 10 cups.*

SWEET RED PEPPER SOUP

THE COUNTRY SQUIRE, NARAMATA, BC / *Owner/Chef: Patt Dyck*

Count on this soup, which uses locally grown sweet red peppers, for a colourful presentation. Be careful not to spill — it stains.

5	tbsp butter
2	large onions, chopped
2	shallots, chopped
4	garlic cloves, crushed
6	sweet red peppers, seeds and membrane removed, chopped
1/2	tsp red pepper flakes
6	cups Double-Strength Chicken Stock* (recipe, page 30)
1 1/3	cups 35% cream
	salt and white pepper
	Tabasco Sauce (optional)
	Cucumber Garnish (recipe follows)

In large heavy-based saucepan, melt butter over medium heat; sauté onions, shallots and garlic, stirring often, for 5 to 8 minutes or until softened. Add red peppers and red pepper flakes to saucepan; cook, stirring, for 3 to 5 minutes. Pour in chicken stock, simmer for 30 minutes.

In food processor, purée soup in batches. Strain and return to saucepan over low heat. Stir in cream and simmer until heated through. Season with salt and pepper to taste. Add dash of Tabasco (if desired). Ladle into bowls; top each with heaping tablespoon of Cucumber Garnish. *Serves 6.*

1/2	English cucumber
1	tsp salt

Cucumber garnish

In food processor, chop cucumber finely. Pour into sieve set over bowl. Sprinkle with salt and let drain for 1 hour. Discard liquid. *Makes 1 1/2 cups.*

SWEET PEA SOUP WITH CRÈME FRAÎCHE AND HAND-PEELED SHRIMP

BEACH SIDE CAFÉ, WEST VANCOUVER, BC / *Executive Chef: Carol Chow*

This chilled soup is truly an all-season recipe. Use fresh peas from your garden or local market in the summer when they are abundant or substitute tender, quick-frozen peas from the supermarket at other times of the year.

2	tbsp butter
1	onion, diced
1	large leek (white part only), thinly sliced
3	cloves garlic, crushed
6	cups chicken stock
2	lb fresh or frozen green peas
	salt and white pepper
1/2	lb cooked shrimp, peeled and deveined
1	cup crème fraîche*

In large saucepan, heat butter over medium heat; sauté onion, leek and garlic for about 5 minutes or until onion is translucent. Add stock and peas; bring to boil. Reduce heat and simmer for 5 minutes or until peas are softened. Remove pan from heat and set in ice bath to cool quickly.

In food processor, purée soup in batches until smooth. Strain through sieve. Season with salt and pepper. Refrigerate until chilled.

Ladle into bowls; garnish with shrimp and dollop of crème fraîche. *Serves 4 to 6.*

Crème fraîche, common to French cookery, is a thickened, smooth cream with a slight acrid, nutty flavour. In France the utilization of unpasteurized cream is common, but we in North America must use pasteurized cream, which lacks the bacteria needed for thickening. Traditional crème fraîche is sold in some specialty markets but is also easy to duplicate at home. In glass bowl, combine 1 cup 35% cream and 2 tbsp buttermilk. Cover and let stand at room temperature for 8 to 24 hours or until thickened. Stir and refrigerate for up to 10 days.

NOGGIN'S CHOWDER

SPINNAKERS BREWPUB & GUESTHOUSE, VICTORIA, BC / *Owner: Paul Hadfield*

Noggin's Chowder has long been a mainstay on the menu at Spinnakers Brewpub. Smooth, creamy, chock-full of seafood and with a hint of dill, it makes a complete meal when served with warm crusty bread. The joy of chowders is that you are not limited to specific seafood but may substitute any fresh fish or shellfish available.

1	clams
5	strips bacon, cut into 1-inch pieces
1	red onion, diced
2	carrots, diced
3	stalks celery, diced
4	cups fish stock
3	potatoes, peeled and cut into 1/2-inch cubes
4	sprigs fresh dill, chopped (or 2 tsp dried dillweed)
	salt and white pepper
1/2	lb scallops
1	lb halibut, cut into 1-inch cubes
1/4	lb smoked salmon, sliced into 1/4-inch strips
1 1/2	cups 10% cream
1	cup 35% cream
1	cup whole milk
2	tsp all-purpose flour
3/4	tsp vegetable oil

Scrub clams, discarding any that have broken shells or do not close when lightly tapped. In large saucepan, bring small amount of water to boil, steam clams for about 5 minutes or until they open. Drain; discard any that have not opened. Set clams aside.

In heavy-based saucepan or Dutch oven, fry bacon until crisp. Drain off excess fat. Add onion, carrots and celery to pan; cook over medium-low heat for 8 to 10 minutes or until softened. Add fish stock, potatoes, dill, and salt and pepper to taste; cover and simmer for 10 to 15 minutes or until vegetables are tender. Add halibut and scallops; cook just until fish turns opaque. Add smoked salmon, clams in shell, 10% cream, 35% cream and milk; heat gently without boiling. Blend flour with oil, whisk into chowder and simmer for 2 minutes or until slightly thickened. Taste and adjust seasoning with salt, pepper and dill if necessary. Ladle into bowls. *Serves 6 generously.*

CAYMAN ISLAND CHOWDER

SALTY'S BEACH HOUSE RESTAURANT, PENTICTON, BC / *Chef: Ken Large*

Chef Ken Large substitutes local Pacific Northwest seafood for the original Caribbean fare in this creation inspired from restaurant owner Rob Wylie's travels to the Cayman Islands. At Salty's the soup base is prepared in advance and fresh seafood is added for individual orders, ensuring that it is cooked to perfection. You may substitute fish and shellfish available to your area.

1	lb combination of Manila clams, mussels and B.C. pink swimming scallops in their shells
1/4	lb lean bacon, diced
1	onion, diced
2	stalks celery, diced
2	cloves garlic, crushed
6	cups water
1	can (28 oz) Italian plum tomatoes
1/2	cup ketchup
2	tbsp dry sherry
1 1/2	tbsp lemon juice
1	tbsp Thai fish sauce*
1	tbsp curry powder (or to taste)
1	tsp Worcestershire sauce
1/4	tsp Tabasco Sauce
1/2	lb salmon, cut in bite-size pieces
1/2	lb halibut, cut in bite-size pieces
1/2	lb shrimp, peeled and deveined

Scrub clams and mussels and remove beards from mussels. Discard any clams or mussels that do not close when tapped. Set aside.

In large heavy-based saucepan over medium heat, sauté bacon until it begins rendering fat. Add onion, celery, and garlic; sauté for 5 minutes or until vegetables are softened and bacon is crisp. Skim excess fat from saucepan if necessary. Add water, tomatoes, ketchup, sherry, lemon juice, fish sauce, curry powder, Worcestershire sauce and Tabasco to saucepan; taste and adjust seasoning. Bring to boil. Reduce heat and simmer for 30 minutes.

Add clams, mussels, scallops, salmon, halibut and shrimp; simmer for about 5 minutes or until fish is just cooked and clams and mussels open. (Discard any that have not opened.) Ladle into bowls. *Serves 6 to 8.*

*Look for Thai fish sauce in specialty sections of supermarkets or in Asian markets.

Chef's wine suggestion: Hester Creek Estate Winery, 1997. Chardonnay Signature Release

INDONESIAN SWEET POTATO, COCONUT AND PEANUT SOUP

RAIN COAST CAFÉ, TOFINO, BC / *Chef de Cuisine: Mark Wrigley*

The influence of Pacific Rim nations on British Columbia cuisine is evident in this sweet exotic Indonesian soup. Chef de Cuisine Mark Wrigley comments that it is one of the most popular items on the cafe's menu, likely due to the aggressive yet complementary flavours. This recipe makes a large quantity. You may reduce it by half, but chef Wrigley suggests that you make the full amount to guarantee leftovers.

1	tbsp vegetable oil
1	large onion, chopped
6	cloves garlic, minced
2	shallots, minced
2	tbsp minced gingerroot
1 1/2	cups water
2 1/2	lb sweet potatoes, diced
1	tsp salt
1/2	tsp pepper
1/2	tsp red pepper flakes
1	cup creamy peanut butter (preferably organic)
1/4	cup tamari*
1	bunch fresh cilantro, chopped
2	cans 15 oz (425 g) coconut milk
	toasted coconut**
	chopped peanuts

In large saucepan, heat oil over medium heat; sauté onion, garlic, shallots and gingerroot, stirring often, for 5 minutes or until softened. Add water, sweet potatoes, salt, pepper and red pepper flakes; bring to boil. Reduce heat to low; cover and simmer potatoes for 20 to 30 minutes or until tender.

Stir in peanut butter, tamari and cilantro. In food processor, purée in batches, pouring in enough of the coconut milk to reach desired consistency.

Return to saucepan and reheat gently; taste and adjust seasoning if necessary. Ladle into bowls; garnish with toasted coconut and chopped peanuts. *Serves 8 to 10.*

*Tamari is a sauce made from soybeans that is similar to soy sauce but thicker and with a distinct mellow flavour. Look for it in the specialty section of supermarkets or in Asian markets.

**To toast coconut, spread on baking sheet and bake in 350ºF oven, stirring often and being careful to prevent burning, for 10 to 12 minutes or until golden.

CREAM OF CHANTERELLE SOUP WITH BLUEBERRY CRÈME FRAÎCHE

RIM ROCK CAFÉ, WHISTLER, BC / *Owner/Chef: Rolf Gunther*

When the lovely trumpet-shaped chanterelle mushroom is in season, Rolf Gunther uses it in this delicately flavoured soup. If unavailable, substitute other mushrooms of choice.

3 tbsp butter
1/2 lb fresh chanterelle mushrooms, chopped
2 shallots, minced
2 cloves garlic, minced
3/4 cup finely diced carrot and celery
1/3 cup dry white wine
1 1/2 cups 35% cream
3 cups vegetable stock (or chicken stock)
salt and pepper
Blueberry Crème Fraîche (recipe follows)
2 to 3 oz smoked trout, thinly sliced

In saucepan, melt butter over medium heat; sauté mushrooms, shallots, garlic, carrot and celery until vegetables are softened. Deglaze pan with wine. Stir in cream and cook, stirring often, until reduced by half. Stir in vegetable stock; season with salt and pepper to taste. Simmer for about 10 minutes or until flavours are blended.

In food processor, purée soup in batches until smooth. Taste and adjust seasoning. Return to saucepan and reheat gently. Ladle into bowls; garnish with dollop of Blueberry Crème Fraîche and smoked trout slices. *Serves 4.*

1/2 cup crème fraîche*
2 tbsp blueberries, puréed

Blueberry Crème Fraîche

Blend together crème fraîche and blueberries until smooth and creamy. *Makes 1/2 cup.*

*If unable to find fresh crème fraîche, make this inexpensive version at home. In glass container combine 1/2 cup 35% cream and 1 tbsp buttermilk. Cover and let stand at room temperature for 12 to 24 hours or until thickened. Stir and refrigerate until ready to use.

HOT-AND-SOUR SOUP

SPINNAKERS BREWPUB & GUESTHOUSE, VICTORIA, BC / *Sous Chef: Dicky Lum*

This variation of a traditional Asian hot-and-sour soup was created by Dicky Lum and features Spinnakers own malt vinegar. Enjoy its tart, tangy, sweet-and-sour flavour.

6	cups beef stock
1/2	cup thinly sliced mushrooms
6	tbsp malt vinegar
1	large tomato, peeled, seeded and slivered
1	tbsp tomato paste
1	tbsp sesame oil
1	tsp brown sugar
1	tsp soy sauce
1/2	tsp Asian chili paste
2	tbsp cornstarch
2	tbsp water
1/2	cup water chestnuts, thinly sliced
2	green onions, cut in 3-inch lengths and slivered
	salt and pepper

In large saucepan, stir together stock, mushrooms, vinegar, tomato, tomato paste, sesame oil, brown sugar, soy sauce and chili sauce; bring to boil. Reduce heat and simmer, stirring occasionally, for 15 minutes. In small bowl, combine cornstarch and water; add to soup and cook, stirring until slightly thickened.

Just before serving, add water chestnuts, and two-thirds of the green onions; season with salt and pepper to taste. Ladle into bowls; garnish with remaining green onions. *Serves 4.*

VICHYSSOISE WITH LOBSTER MEDALLIONS

LE CROCODILE, VANCOUVER, BC / *Owner/Chef: Michel Jacob*

Chef Michel Jacob prepares this very delicate, smooth chilled soup in the traditional French manner but with an addition of lobster medallions and garnish of tobiko eggs and fresh herbs.

2	tbsp butter
1	medium onion, diced
1	medium leek, chopped
1	lb Yukon gold potatoes, peeled and diced
1	clove garlic, minced
1	bouquet garni (parsley, thyme and bay leaves tied in cheesecloth bag)
2	cups vegetable stock (or chicken stock)
1/2	cup 35% cream
1/4	cup spinach mousse*
1	whole lobster tail, poached
2	tsp tobiko eggs
2	tsp each chopped fresh chives and parsley

In large saucepan, heat butter over medium heat; sauté onion for 5 minutes or until softened. Add leek, potatoes, garlic and bouquet garni; pour in vegetable stock. Cover and simmer for 1 hour. Remove bouquet garni and simmer for 30 minutes longer.

In food processor, purée soup in batches. If necessary strain through sieve to remove stringy portions. Cover and refrigerate until chilled.

Just before serving, stir in cream and spinach mousse. Slice lobster tail crosswise and add to soup. Ladle into bowls; garnish with tobiko eggs, parsley and chives. *Serves 4.*

*Le Crocodile uses a spinach mousse in this recipe but you can substitute 1/4 cup cooked spinach that has been puréed and passed through a sieve.

Chef's wine suggestion: Napa Valley Duckhorn Sauvignon Blanc

SMOKED GOUDA SOUP

THE MAHLE HOUSE RESTAURANT, NANAIMO, BC / *Owner/Chef: Maureen Loucks*

Warm up on winter days with this rich, smoky cheese soup. It would also work well as a cheese fondue served with crusty French bread cubes; simply reduce a little longer during the simmering stage.

1/4	cup butter
1	large onion, chopped
2	tsp minced garlic
1	tbsp all-purpose flour
6	cups chicken stock
	salt and white pepper
2	cups 35% cream
8	oz shredded smoked Gouda cheese
	chopped fresh chives or basil

In saucepan, melt butter over medium-low heat; sweat onion until translucent. Add garlic and cook, stirring often, for 2 minutes. Whisk in flour; cook, stirring constantly, for 1 minute. Stir in chicken stock and season with salt and pepper to taste; bring to boil. Reduce heat and simmer, stirring frequently, for 30 to 45 minutes. Stir in cream and cook, stirring often, until reduced slightly. Stir in cheese until melted and smooth.

In food processor, purée soup in batches. Strain and return to saucepan; reheat gently. Ladle into bowls; garnish with chives or basil. *Serves 6.*

CARROT AND SAGE VELOUTÉ

THE AERIE RESORT, MALAHAT, BC / *Chef de Cuisine: Chris Jones, Sous-Chef: Christophe Letard*

Caramelized carrots give this soup its warm golden colour and rich flavour. Accompanied by fresh biscuits or warm crusty rolls, it is the ideal meal-in-a-bowl for the chilling days of autumn and winter.

1 1/2	lb carrots, sliced
2	tbsp olive oil
1	onion, diced
6	cloves garlic, minced
3	stalks celery, diced
1	bay leaf
5	whole peppercorns
2	cups Riesling
3 to 4	cups chicken stock
1/4	cup arborio rice
1	tbsp chopped fresh sage (or 1 tsp dried)
	10% cream (optional)
	fresh sage sprigs

In bowl, toss carrots with half of the oil; transfer to roasting pan and bake in 350°F oven for about 45 minutes or until tender and caramelized. In large heavy-based saucepan, heat remaining oil over medium heat; sauté onion, garlic, celery, bay leaf and peppercorns until onions are softened and smell sweet. Add wine and cook, stirring often, until reduced by two-thirds.

Add roasted carrots, chicken stock, rice and chopped sage to pan; bring to boil. Reduce heat and simmer, stirring occasionally, for 25 minutes. Remove bay leaf.

In food processor, purée soup in batches. Pass through sieve. Reheat gently, adding additional stock or 10% cream if necessary to reach desired consistency. Ladle into bowls and sprinkle with sage sprigs. *Serves 6.*

PACIFIC OYSTER STEW

SEASONS RESTAURANT IN QUEEN ELIZABETH PARK, VANCOUVER, BC / *Executive Chef: Pierre Delacote*

There are some who claim that the oyster is an aphrodisiac, but don't let that be the only reason to savour this delicate but rich soup. Its elegant presentation also makes a stunning first course when entertaining. If you are unable to find local Fanny Bay oysters, substitute fresh oysters of your choice.

1/4	cup unsalted butter
1	medium leek (white part only), julienned
1/4	cup dry white wine
1 2/3	cups 35% cream
20	fresh-shucked Fanny Bay oysters with juice
	salt
	freshly cracked black pepper

In shallow skillet, heat butter over medium heat; sauté leek, stirring for about 20 seconds, being careful not to brown. With slotted spoon, remove leek and set aside on plate. Deglaze skillet with wine. Add cream and oysters with juice; bring to rolling boil. With slotted spoon, remove oysters and divide equally among 4 very hot soup plates. Return sauce to boil; reduce for a few seconds and season with salt to taste. Ladle sauce over oysters; top with leeks and finish with freshly cracked black pepper. *Serves 4.*

SALADS

IN TODAY'S WORLD, THE TERM "SALAD" CAN MEAN ANYTHING FROM A MIX OF SIMPLE GREENS DRIZZLED WITH A BASIC vinaigrette to an elaborate main-course dish that includes all food groups. The choice is yours to dress up or down according to your inclination.

The contributing chefs have provided a wide variety of recipes featuring the joining of their culinary backgrounds with the local produce of the region. You are guaranteed to find a number of recipes to add to your permanent collection in these ingenious offerings.

Many of the recipes, such as Sunomono Salad from The Grotto Restaurant in Nanaimo, demonstrate the strong Asian influence in West Coast cuisine. There are a number of interesting warm salads, including Cellar Door Bistro's Cellar Door Caesar, a unique variation on the traditional Caesar salad.

When fresh garden beans are in season, try The Amphora Bistro's Green and Yellow Bean Salad with Warm Bacon Vinaigrette, which showcases fresh Okanagan Valley produce.

Salads provide an ideal opportunity to promote healthier eating. Use olive and canola oils, which are the highest in monounsaturated fats of all oils, and when possible, serve dressings on the side to allow individuals to add only the desired amount.

◀ Edgewater Salad

EDGEWATER SALAD

EDGEWATER LODGE, WHISTLER, BC / *Executive Chef: Thomas Piekarski*

Chef Piekarski, who garnishes his house salad of organic greens and vegetables with edible flowers, describes it as "a visually pleasing array of seasonal greens and tomatoes, enlivened by a simple lemon, herb, garlic and olive oil dressing." The variety of garden vegetables in this recipe is extensive; you may want to substitute greens of choice if any are unavailable.

	salad greens and vegetables to serve 4 to 6 (e.g. sorrel, pea tips, arugula, ruby chard, kale, mizuna, fava tips)
2	green onions, sliced
1/2	sweet red pepper, julienned
1/2	sweet green pepper, julienned
1/2	sweet yellow pepper, julienned
1	large or 2 small tomatoes, cut in wedges
1/4	cup chopped fresh parsley
	Balsamic Sesame Vinaigrette (recipe follows)
	garnish of edible flowers (e.g. pansies, rose petals, violets, daisies, geraniums, marigolds, nasturtiums)*

In large bowl, combine salad greens and vegetables, green onions, red, green and yellow peppers, tomatoes and parsley; toss with Balsamic Sesame Vinaigrette just to coat. Arrange salad on chilled salad plates and garnish with edible flowers. *Serves 4 to 6.*

*use only flowers that are pesticide free.

Balsamic Sesame Vinaigrette

1/2	cup balsamic vinegar
2	tbsp brown sugar
1/4	cup olive oil
1/4	cup sesame oil
1	large clove garlic, minced
1	tbsp lemon juice
	salt and pepper
1/2	cup vegetable oil

In blender, mix balsamic vinegar and brown sugar for 1 minute. With blender running, add olive and sesame oils in slow steady stream, blending until smooth. Mix in garlic, lemon juice, and salt and pepper to taste. With blender running, add vegetable oil in slow steady stream, blending until bonded and silky. *Makes 1 1/2 cups.*

Chef's wine suggestion: crisp Chardonnay of choice

GREEN AND YELLOW BEAN SALAD WITH A WARM BACON VINAIGRETTE

THE AMPHORA BISTRO AT HAINLE VINEYARDS ESTATE WINERY, PEACHLAND, BC / *Executive Chef: David Forestell*

This decidedly different salad features Okanagan Valley produce. The string beans, cubed potatoes and delicious apple cider and mustard vinaigrette make a hearty salad that can readily be served as a luncheon entrée.

1	lb Blue Lake or other green beans, trimmed
3/4	lb yellow wax beans, trimmed
1/2	cup fresh chives, cut in 2-inch lengths
1/4	cup coarsely chopped Italian parsley
1/4	cup coarsely chopped celery leaves
1/2	lb bacon, diced
1	cup Yellow Finn or German Fingerling or other yellow fleshed potatoes, peeled and cut into 1/4-inch cubes
1/2	cup thinly sliced shallots
4	cloves garlic, minced
1/4	cup grainy Dijon mustard
1/3	cup organic apple cider (hard or soft)
1/3	cup organic apple cider vinegar
1/2	cup olive oil
	salt and pepper
2	cups coarsely chopped yellow tomatoes (optional)

In pot of boiling salted water blanch green and yellow beans for about 3 to 4 minutes or until al dente. Plunge beans immediately into cold water to stop cooking; drain and place in large serving bowl. Add chives, parsley and celery leaves; stir to combine. Set aside.

In heavy skillet, cook bacon over medium heat until crisp. With slotted spoon, transfer to paper towel to drain. Drain all but 3 tbsp fat from skillet. Return skillet to medium-high heat; cook potatoes for 2 to 3 minutes or until starting to brown. Add shallots; cook, stirring often, for 2 to 3 minutes or until lightly browned. Add garlic; cook, stirring often, for 1 to 2 minutes.

Stir in mustard; cook, stirring, for a few minutes or until moisture is almost evaporated. Pour in cider and cider vinegar and increase heat to high; cook until volume is reduced by half. Stir in bacon. Remove from heat; lightly whisk in olive oil until well blended. Season with salt and pepper to taste.

While dressing is still warm, pour over vegetable mixture; toss to combine. Let stand for 15 minutes before serving. Add tomatoes (if using) just before serving. *Serves 6 to 8.*

Chef's wine suggestion: Pinot Blanc, Pinot Gris or lightly oaked Chardonnay

SPINNAKERS MIXED GREENS WITH RASPBERRY VINAIGRETTE

SPINNAKERS BREWPUB & GUESTHOUSE, VICTORIA, BC / Owner: Paul Hadfield

Spinnakers likes to highlight products made on the premises. This rosy, semisweet vinaigrette features the restaurant's special malt vinegar, which may be purchased on site. You can substitute malt vinegar of your choice.

1	lb mixed salad greens
	Raspberry Vinaigrette (recipe follows)

Arrange salad loosely on plates and drizzle with Raspberry Vinaigrette. *Serves 4.*

Raspberry Vinaigrette

2	cups water
2/3	cup fresh raspberries
1/4	cup granulated sugar
1/4	cups chopped fresh basil
2	tbsp malt vinegar
1 1/2	tbsp Dijon mustard
1	clove garlic, crushed
1	cup olive oil
	salt and pepper

In small saucepan, combine water, raspberries, sugar and basil; bring to boil. Cook, stirring, until reduced by half. Pass through sieve into bowl to remove seeds. Let cool.

In blender, purée raspberry juice, vinegar, mustard and garlic. With machine running, add oil in slow steady stream, blending until emulsified. Season with salt and pepper to taste. *Makes 1 1/2 cups.*

SPICY MESCLUN WITH AVOCADO, MANGO AND STILTON CHEESE

THE LATCH COUNTRY INN, SIDNEY, BC / *Owner/Chef: Heidi Rust*

Mesclun is a mix of young salad greens and is sold in the specialty section of most produce departments. The mix may vary but will commonly include arugula, oak leaf, radicchio, sorrel, frisée and dandelion. Chef Heidi Rust suggests that for a slight variation of flavour you can also use feta or goat cheese instead of the Stilton.

mesclun mix to serve 6
1 avocado, peeled and thinly sliced
1 ripe mango, peeled and thinly sliced
4 oz Stilton cheese, crumbled
Balsamic Vinaigrette (recipe follows)

Wash and thoroughly dry mesclun. Arrange attractively on 6 large plates; top with avocado and mango slices. Sprinkle with Stilton; drizzle with Balsamic Vinaigrette. *Serves 6.*

1/4 cup balsamic vinegar
2 tbsp chopped fresh basil
1 tbsp Dijon mustard
1 large clove garlic, minced
1 tsp grated gingerroot
1 cup olive oil
salt and pepper

Balsamic Vinaigrette

Whisk together vinegar, basil, mustard, garlic and ginger. In slow steady stream, whisk in olive oil until emulsified. Season with salt and pepper to taste. *Makes 1 1/3 cups.*

Innkeeper's wine suggestion: Mission Hill Private Reserve Gewürztraminer VQA

CAPRESE SALAD OF TOMATOES AND BOCCONCINI

BORGO ANTICO RISTORANTE, VANCOUVER, BC / *Owner: Umberto Menghi*

Not only does this salad taste very Italian, it also takes on the colours of Italy. Like the stripes of the national flag, ripe red Roma tomatoes, creamy white bocconcini cheese and green basil combine for an Italian-style experience.

1/2	cup balsamic vinegar
	pinch granulated sugar
4	Roma tomatoes, sliced
	salt and pepper
4	balls buffalo bocconcini* sliced
	finely chopped fresh basil leaves
4	tbsp extra-virgin olive oil

In saucepan over medium heat, stir vinegar with sugar; cook, stirring often, until reduced by one-quarter. Set aside and let cool.

TO SERVE: On each of 4 salad plates, arrange tomato slices in circle; season lightly with salt and pepper. Top with bocconcini slices; garnish with fresh basil leaves. Drizzle balsamic reduction around perimeter of plates and olive oil on top of bocconcini. *Serves 4.*

Bocconcini are small balls of fresh mozzarella that are usually packed in water or whey. Use regular cow's milk bocconcini if buffalo are not available.

CAMBOZOLA CALDO CON CROSTINI

TRATTORIA DI UMBERTO RESTAURANT, WHISTLER, BC / *Owner: Umberto Menghi*

Crostini means "little toasts" in Italian, and this version, topped with tomato and roasted garlic, makes a wonderful accompaniment to a salad of lightly dressed greens and hot Cambozola cheese. The Rockies may surround the restaurant but the aroma is pure Alps!

8	slices French stick (baguette), sliced on diagonal 3/8 inch thick
4	tomatoes
6	cloves roasted garlic, minced
	mixed greens to serve 6
2	oz Cambazola cheese, sliced 1/2 inch thick
1	tbsp extra-virgin olive oil
1	tbsp balsamic vinegar

Toast bread in 375°F oven until lightly browned; set aside.

Slice tomatoes in half. Hold each half in palm of hand, extract juices and seeds; dice. In bowl, combine diced tomato and garlic; spread on toasted bread. Set aside.

Place sliced Cambozola on baking sheet and broil for about 1 minute or until browned.

Meanwhile, in bowl, whisk together olive oil and balsamic vinegar. Add greens and toss to coat.

TO SERVE: Arrange greens in the centre of large platter. Arrange crostini around outside of platter. Top with Cambozola. May also be served on individual salad plates as seen in photo. *Serves 4.*

Wine suggestion: Sumac Ridge Sauvignon Blanc VQA, 1998

SUNOMONO SALAD

THE GROTTO, NANAIMO, BC / *Owner: Mike Yoshida, Chef: Dave Armour*

Chef Dave Armour suggests serving this refreshing salad as a first course or luncheon entrée on a hot summer's day. For a variation, you can substitute 1/4 lb Dungeness crab for the shrimp.

4	oz dried yam noodles*
	vegetable oil
	Boston or Bibb lettuce to serve 4
1/2	cucumber, peeled, seeded and julienned
1	Granny Smith apple, cored, peeled and sliced
1/2	lb cooked shrimp, peeled and deveined
1/2	tsp lemon juice
	Sunomono Dressing (recipe follows)

In pot of boiling water cook noodles for 2 to 4 minutes or until al dente; drain and rinse under cold running water. Transfer noodles to bowl; toss with small amount of vegetable oil to keep from sticking. Cover and refrigerate until chilled.

In large bowl, combine noodles, lettuce, cucumber, apple and shrimp; toss with lemon juice. Lightly coat salad with Sunomono Dressing; toss and serve on chilled salad plates. *Serves 4.*

*Asian noodles are made from a variety of sources: wheat, rice, soy, yam, etc. If unable to find yam noodles, substitute 1 1/2 pkg ramen noodles.

1/4	cup mirin (Japanese rice wine)
1	tbsp granulated sugar
2	tsp soy sauce
1	tsp grated gingerroot
1	tsp lemon juice

Sunomono Dressing

In small bowl, whisk together mirin, sugar, soy sauce, gingerroot and lemon juice until sugar is dissolved. *Makes 1/3 cup.*

CELLAR DOOR CAESAR

CELLAR DOOR BISTRO & CATERING, SUMMERLAND, BC / *Chef: Dana Reinhardt*

How delightfully different — Caesar salad with grilled romaine lettuce! The presentation is unique and the taste is exceptional.

1	tbsp grainy Dijon mustard
1 1/2	tsp minced garlic
1	tsp Thai fish sauce*
1/2	tsp pepper, freshly ground
1/4	tsp Worcestershire sauce
1	cold egg yolk
3/4	cup vegetable oil
2 1/2	tbsp lemon juice
2	heads romaine lettuce, outer leaves removed
1/2	cup shredded Asiago cheese
	Herbed Croutons (recipe follows)

In food processor, combine mustard, garlic, fish sauce, pepper, Worcestershire sauce and egg yolk; purée until smooth. With machine running, add oil in slow steady stream, processing until thickened. Add lemon juice; pulse to combine. Cover and set aside in refrigerator.

Heat grill to 400° to 450°F. Cut romaine into quarters if large and into thirds if small. Spray both sides with light coating of vegetable oil and place on hot grill; char leaves slightly on both sides. To serve: Arrange on large dinner plates. Drizzle dressing along length of romaine; top with Asiago cheese and Herbed Croutons. *Serves 6 to 8.*

*Thai fish sauce is sold in the specialty section of most supermarkets.

1/2	loaf good-quality peasant bread
1 to 2	tbsp vegetable oil
1/2	tsp minced garlic
1	tbsp chopped fresh herbs (basil, chives, thyme)
1	tbsp butter, melted
	sea salt and pepper

Herbed Croutons

Cut bread into 1-inch cubes. Heat skillet over medium heat and coat bottom of pan with oil; cook bread cubes for 4 to 5 minutes, turning to brown on all sides. Add garlic, herbs and melted butter; toss with croutons to coat. Season with salt and pepper to taste. *Makes 4 to 5 cups croutons.*

SPINACH SALAD WITH HONEY DRESSING AND PANCETTA FETA TUQUES

LA RUA RESTAURANTE, WHISTLER, BC / *Executive Chef: Tim Muehlbauer*

Chef Tim Muehlbauer creates a new twist on the traditional spinach salad. The honey dressing is sweet but not overpowering, and his broiled Italian bacon and goat cheese "hat" tops off the salad in an unique way.

4	slices pancetta*
3 oz	feta cheese, crumbled
1 lb	fresh spinach, trimmed and torn
	Honey Dressing (recipe follows)
8	cultivated white mushroom caps, sliced
1	small bunch fresh parsley, chopped
2	hard-cooked eggs, finely chopped

Place slices of pancetta on baking sheet; sprinkle with feta. Set aside.

In large salad bowl, toss spinach with small amount of Honey Dressing to moisten. Add mushrooms and half of the chopped parsley; toss.

Broil pancetta "tuques" under broiler until golden, being careful to watch that cheese does not burn.

TO SERVE: Arrange spinach in centre of serving dishes; drizzle with remaining honey dressing if desired. Garnish with egg and remaining parsley; top with panchetta "tuque." *Serves 4.*

*Pancetta (cured Italian bacon) is available in the deli section of most supermarkets or Italian grocery stores.

1	cup white wine
1/3	cup minced shallots
1/3	cup liquid honey
4	tsp raspberry vinegar
1	tsp Dijon mustard
1	tsp lemon juice
	pinch ground cardamom
4	tbsp vegetable oil (or flavoured oil of choice)

Honey Dressing

In small saucepan over medium-high heat, cook wine and shallots for 12 to 15 minutes or until reduced to syrupy consistency.

In bowl, whisk together wine mixture, honey, vinegar, Dijon mustard, lemon juice and cardamom. Gradually whisk in oil until emulsified. *Makes 1 cup.*

ENTRÉES

THERE ARE SO MANY MEATS TO CHOOSE FROM AND SO MANY WAYS TO PREPARE THEM, I FOUND MYSELF WONDERING HOW I could possibly narrow the selection for a well-rounded cookbook. I decided the best course of action was simply to ask the chefs to contribute their favourite meat entrées. Presto! The solution of what to include was in their replies.

In this section you will find a superb variety of recipes encompassing beef, pork, chicken, game, veal and lamb. All the recipes are innovative and represent the best of local ingredients. Edgewater Marinated Venison Medallions from chef Thomas Piekarski in Whistler and Chanterelle-Stuffed Venison Medallions from The Herald St. Caffe in Victoria feature farm-raised venison that melts in your mouth. Chicken is prepared in a variety of ways, including a curry, a coq-au-vin and breasts stuffed with smoked salmon. Two of the chefs showed their partiality for pork and responded with recipes for pork tenderloin with fruit and ribs Asian-style.

Whether you are a novice or a seasoned cook, you will find numerous recipes in this section suited to your range of expertise. Many are ideal for family-style meals while others are perfect for entertaining.

◀ Cinnamon Chili Rub Flank Steak

CINNAMON CHILI RUB FLANK STEAK

BIN 941 TAPAS PARLOUR, VANCOUVER, BC / *Owner/Chef: Gord Martin*

Do not be overwhelmed by the combination of ingredients in this Pacific Northwest adaptation of a southern Texan dish. The result is simply delicious. At BIN 941 this "tapatiser" is served with black pepper pommes frites but the chef says you can also accompany the dish with whipped mashed potatoes or rice and fresh seasonal vegetables. Chef Martin cautions that you should cook flank steak only to rare as overcooking toughens it.

1/3	cup chili powder
2	tbsp cinnamon
	pinch salt
	pepper
2	lb flank steak
1 to 2	tsp olive oil
1/2	cup beef stock
1/4	cup liquid honey
1	tbsp canned chipotle pepper, puréed
1	tbsp unsalted butter

In bowl, combine chili powder, cinnamon, salt and generous amount of pepper. Trim steak and lightly score in a crosshatch fashion on both sides. Rub chili mixture into steak; place in large resealable plastic bag and marinate in refrigerator for at least 2 hours or for up to preferred 24 hours.

In skillet, heat oil over high heat; sear steaks for about 3 minutes per side just until rare. Transfer to plate and let stand. Return skillet to high heat; deglaze pan with stock. Add honey and chipotle pepper; reduce, stirring often, until thickened. Whisk butter into sauce; remove from heat and strain.

TO SERVE: Thinly slice steak across the grain and drizzle with sauce. *Serves 4 to 6.*

SMOKED PORK TENDERLOIN WITH OVEN-DRIED DAMSON PLUMS

CELLAR DOOR BISTRO & CATERING, SUMMERLAND, BC / *Chef: Dana Reinhardt*

At the Cellar Door Bistro, the chef hot-smokes tenderloins briefly — 4 to 6 minutes depending on size — with vine cuttings from the vineyard. If you do not have a smoker, purchase the tenderloins at specialty meat markets or use regular tenderloins. Prepare Oven-Dried Damson Plums in advance.

2	pork tenderloins, each 1 to 1 1/2 lb
2	tbsp freshly cracked pepper
1 1/2	tbsp vegetable oil
2	tbsp minced shallots
1	tbsp chopped fresh thyme
2/3	cup Merlot
2/3	cup brown stock
1	cup Oven-Dried Damson Plums (recipe follows)
	salt and pepper

Trim any fat from tenderloins; tuck tail under so meat is of uniform thickness, tying with kitchen string if necessary. If smoking, prepare hot-smoker with grapevine cuttings or other scented wood, such as applewood. For 1 lb tenderloins hotsmoke for 4 minutes, 1 1/2 lb tenderloins 6 minutes. Remove tenderloins and pat dry.

Sprinkle pepper on sheet of waxed paper; lightly roll tenderloins in pepper to coat. Shake off excess. In large heavy-based skillet, heat oil over medium-high heat; sear tenderloins on each side and transfer to ovenproof baking dish. Bake in 425°F oven for 12 to 15 minutes or until internal temperature reaches 160°F or until juices run clear when pork is pierced and just a hint of pink remains inside. Let stand for 10 minutes.

Meanwhile, return skillet used to sear pork to medium-high heat; briefly sauté shallots and thyme. Deglaze skillet with wine, stirring often, for about 8 minutes or until reduced to syrup. Add brown stock and Oven-Dried Damson Plums and reduce to consistency of sauce. Season with salt and pepper to taste.

TO SERVE: Slice tenderloins into 1 1/2-inch thick medallions and spoon plum sauce over top. *Serves 6.*

1 1/2	lb Damson plums (or plums of choice)
2	tsp granulated sugar

Oven-Dried Damson Plums

Slice plums in half and discard pits. Line large baking sheet with parchment paper and place plums, cut side up, on sheet; sprinkle with sugar. Bake in 170°F oven for about 3 hours or until plums have shrunk by half. Let cool. Transfer to plate and set aside. *Makes 1 cup.*

Chef's wine suggestion: Stags Hollow Merlot or Nichol Vineyards Syrah

CHANTERELLE-STUFFED VENISON MEDALLIONS WITH THREE-PEPPERCORN SOY VINAIGRETTE

HERALD STREET CAFFE, VICTORIA, BC / *Executive Chef: Mark Finnigan*

Mark Finnigan prefers to use fresh local organic produce and meats in his food preparation at the Herald Street Caffe. This recipe, featuring British Columbia venison, offers a delicious "hint of the wild" in a refined setting. Prepare pâté and peppercorn sauce one day in advance.

2 1/4	lb fresh venison, cut in 6-oz medallions
	Chanterelle Pâté (recipe follows)
1 to 2	tsp vegetable oil
	Three-Peppercorn Soy Vinaigrette (recipe follows)
2	tbsp butter

Make horizontal slit in side of each medallion to form small pocket. Fill each medallion with 2 to 3 oz pâté; let stand for 1 hour.

In skillet, heat oil over medium-high heat; sear medallions, turning once. Transfer to baking sheet and bake in 425°F oven for 6 to 8 minutes or until medium-rare.

Meanwhile, heat prepared peppercorn sauce in same skillet over low heat; add butter and cook until reduced to a shiny glaze. Remove from heat and keep warm.

TO SERVE: Place medallions on warmed plates and drizzle with Three-Peppercorn Soy Vinaigrette. *Serves 6.*

Chanterelle Pâté

1	tsp vegetable oil
1	tsp butter
1	leek (white part only), sliced
1	cup fresh chanterelle mushrooms
1	cup white mushrooms
1	cup bread crumbs
3/4	cup chestnut purée*
2	tbsp Madeira
1	tsp dried sage
	pinch each salt and pepper

In skillet, heat oil and butter over medium heat; sauté leek and mushrooms until golden. Stir in bread crumbs, chestnut purée, wine, sage and season with salt and pepper to taste.

Transfer mixture to food processor; process until smooth. Refrigerate until ready to use. *Makes 2 1/2 cups.*

*Chestnut purée is available in the specialty section of supermarkets.

Three-Peppercorn Soy Vinaigrette

1	cup white wine
1/2	cup packed brown sugar
1/2	cup soy sauce
1	tsp minced garlic
1	tsp grated gingerroot
2 to 3	tbsp cracked black, green and pink peppercorns

In small saucepan over medium heat, combine wine, sugar, soy sauce, garlic, ginger and peppercorns; simmer, stirring often, for 15 minutes. Remove from heat and let cool. Refrigerate until ready to use. *Makes 1 1/2 cups.*

Chef's wine suggestion: California Cabernet Sauvignon

ROASTED GARLIC CHICKEN
AND GRILLED VEGETABLES

IL GIARDINO AND UMBERTO'S, VANCOUVER, BC / *Owner: Umberto Menghi*

This recipe turns an ordinary roast chicken entrée into a delicious medley of Mediterranean flavours and aromas with the addition of grilled vegetables infused with rosemary and thyme.

3 to 4	lb whole chicken
	salt and pepper
10	sprigs fresh thyme
1 1/2	tbsp extra-virgin olive oil
4	large garlic cloves, skins on
	Grilled Vegetables (recipe follows)

Remove all visible fat from chicken; wash inside and out and dry with paper towels. Lightly season chicken cavity with salt and pepper; stuff with thyme. Spread oil evenly over chicken skin. Place chicken and garlic cloves in cast-iron skillet; bake in 375°F oven, basting every 15 minutes with pan juices, for 1 1/4 to 1 1/2 hours or until meat thermometer registers 185°F. Let stand for 10 minutes before carving.

TO SERVE: Place Grilled Vegetables on large warmed platter. Arrange chicken pieces and garlic over vegetables. *Serves 4 to 6.*

1/4	cup extra-virgin olive oil
2	sprigs fresh rosemary, chopped
1	tbsp chopped fresh thyme
2	sweet red or green peppers
2	zucchini
1	eggplant
4	tomatoes

Grilled Vegetables

In shallow dish stir together oil, rosemary and thyme. Let stand for 30 minutes or until flavours are blended. Cut peppers in half lengthwise and remove seeds; in pot of boiling water, blanch peppers for 2 minutes. Drain. Cut peppers and zucchini in large strips and eggplant and tomatoes in 1/4-inch slices; brush vegetables with flavoured oil.

Transfer vegetables to greased grill over medium-high heat; cook for 4 to 8 minutes, turning often, or until al dente. Remove individual slices as they reach desired doneness and keep warm.

Chef's wine suggestion: Sumac Ridge Meritage VQA, 1996

CHICKEN CURRY

BENGAL LOUNGE AT THE EMPRESS HOTEL, VICTORIA, BC / *Executive Chef: David Hammonds*

The Empress Hotel was named in honour of Queen Victoria, the ruling matriarch of the British Commonwealth when the hotel opened in 1908. In keeping with its British colonial heritage, the Bengal Lounge features an à la carte menu and curry luncheon buffet with an East Indian flavour. Serve with basmati rice and assorted condiments and chutneys, such as the Mount Currie Rhubarb and Sweet Ginger Chutney found on page 113.

3	tbsp vegetable oil
2	tsp minced garlic
2	tsp minced gingerroot
4	lb chicken pieces (legs, thighs, breasts), skin removed
2	tbsp medium curry powder
2	bay leaves
2	tsp ground cumin
1	tsp ground coriander
1	tsp turmeric
1	cup chicken stock
1/2	cup chopped onion
1/2	cup chopped celery
1/2	cup chopped carrot
1/2	cup chopped tomato
1	apple, peeled, cored and diced
2	tbsp tomato paste
2	tbsp lemon juice
	salt and pepper

In large ovenproof saucepan heat oil over medium-high heat; cook garlic and ginger for 1 to 2 minutes. Brown chicken on all sides. Transfer to plate and set aside.

Add curry powder, bay leaves, cumin, coriander and turmeric to saucepan; sauté, stirring, for 1 minute, being careful not to burn. Add stock, onion, celery, carrots, tomato, apple, tomato paste, lemon juice, and salt and pepper to taste; bring to boil. Reduce heat and simmer, stirring often, for 5 minutes. Return chicken pieces to saucepan; cover and bake in 375°F oven for 30 minutes, turning the chicken occasionally. Uncover and cook for 5 minutes longer. *Serves 4.*

COQ AU VIN WITH BRAISED GREENS

THE AMPHORA RESTAURANT AT HAINLE VINEYARDS ESTATE WINERY, PEACHLAND, BC / *Executive Chef: David Forestell*

Chef David Forestell's bold use of unusual herbs and spices in this traditional French recipe will fill your kitchen with inviting aromas on a cool autumn or winter day. Serve the dish over a bed of noodles.

1/2	lb lean bacon, finely chopped
8	shallots or pearl onions, peeled
2	onions, diced
1/4	cup liquid honey
2	tbsp coarsely ground pepper
3 to 4	lb chicken pieces (legs, thighs, breasts) skin removed and trimmed of fat salt and pepper
1	can (28 oz) crushed Italian plum tomatoes
2	cups chicken stock
1	bottle (750 ml) Pinot Noir wine
3	bay leaves
4	sprigs savory (or 1/2 tsp dried)
6	juniper berries
1	whole clove
3	star anise*
1/2	cinnamon stick
1/2	orange, cut in 2 wedges
1	lb fall greens (kale, rhubarb chard, mustard or beet in a combination), washed and coarsely chopped

In large heavy-based ovenproof saucepan, cook bacon over medium-high heat until crisp. With slotted spoon, transfer to large bowl and set aside. Drain all but 2 tbsp fat from pan; sauté shallots and onions over medium-high heat for 2 to 3 minutes or until beginning to brown. Add honey and pepper; cook for about 15 minutes or until onions are caramelized. Add onions to bacon in bowl.

Season chicken pieces with salt and pepper. In same pan on high heat, brown chicken in batches, adding additional bacon fat if necessary to prevent sticking. Remove and add to bacon and onion. Add tomatoes and stock to pan and cook over medium-high heat, stirring occasionally, until liquid is reduced to one-quarter of its volume. Add wine to pan along with reserved chicken, onions and bacon; bring to boil. Remove from heat. Add bay leaves, savory, juniper berries, clove, star anise, cinnamon stick and orange wedges; cover and bake in 350°F oven for 1 1/2 hours or until liquid is reduced and thickened sufficiently to add "shine" to chicken. (Dish can be prepared to this point up to 24 hours in advance, covered and refrigerated; reheat in oven.)

About 15 minutes before serving, poke greens into liquid around chicken and return pan to oven. Before serving, remove bay leaves, star anise, cinnamon stick and orange segments. *Serves 4 to 6.*

*Found in Asian Food stores and some supermarkets.

Chef's wine suggestions: a topnotch Pinot Noir

HERB-CRUSTED RACK OF LAMB

THE TEAHOUSE RESTAURANT IN STANLEY PARK, VANCOUVER, BC / *Executive Chef: Lynda Larouche*

French-style roasted rack of lamb is a classy entrée to serve guests or family for a special occasion. If you are lucky, you will be able to obtain fresh local lamb, but if not, purchase frozen New Zealand lamb from the frozen foods section of your supermarket. Honey Wine Sauce is a delicious accompaniment and is equally good with grilled steak.

1/2	cup bread crumbs
1	tbsp each chopped fresh rosemary, thyme and parsley (or 1 tsp each dried)
1	tbsp minced garlic
1	tbsp butter
2	racks of lamb, each 12 to 14 oz
1	tbsp vegetable oil
1/4	cup Dijon mustard
	salt and pepper
	Honey Wine Sauce (recipe follows)

In bowl, combine bread crumbs, rosemary, thyme, parsley, garlic and butter; set aside. Trim any fat from lamb.

In ovenproof skillet or roasting pan heat oil over medium-high heat; briefly sear lamb racks on both sides. Remove from heat. Brush lamb with mustard; season with salt and pepper to taste. Press crumb mixture into meaty side of lamb. Bake in 375°F oven for 25 to 30 minutes for rare, or until desired doneness. Remove from oven and let stand for 5 minutes.

TO SERVE: Slice lamb between bones. Pour Honey Wine Sauce in centre of warmed plates. Arrange 3 to 4 ribs per serving on pool of sauce. *Serves 4.*

1	cup dry white wine
1/2	cup 35% cream
1	tbsp minced shallot
1	tsp liquid honey
1	tbsp cornstarch
1	tsp water

Honey Wine Sauce

In small saucepan, whisk together wine, cream, shallot and honey; bring to boil. Reduce heat to low. Whisk cornstarch with water and whisk into sauce; cook, whisking, until thickened. Remove from heat and keep warm. *Makes 1 cup.*

SMOKED SALMON–STUFFED CHICKEN BREAST IN PHYLLO WITH SOUR CHERRY GINGER GLAZE

GOOD LIFE BOOKSTORE CAFÉ, SOOKE, BC / *Owner/Executive Chef: Ricardo Monteiro*

This entrée — smoked salmon stuffed in succulent chicken and wrapped in crunchy phyllo — takes a little more time to prepare but the result is well worth the effort. Chef Monteiro uses sour cherries for the glaze when they are available in the spring, but you may substitute other berries and fruits in season.

2	tsp olive oil
3	oz hickory-smoked salmon, chopped
3	oz spinach, blanched and chopped
3	oz fresh wild mushrooms of choice, sliced (or regular button mushrooms, sliced)
1/2	tsp dried basil
1/2	tsp dried thyme
1/2	tsp dried oregano
	salt and pepper
4	boneless skinless chicken breasts, each 6 oz
8	sheets phyllo pastry
1/4	cup butter, melted
	Sour Cherry Ginger Glaze (recipe follows)

In skillet, heat oil over medium heat; sauté salmon, spinach, mushrooms, basil, thyme and oregano, stirring for about 4 minutes or until mushrooms are softened and flavours are blended. Season with salt and pepper to taste. Let cool and set aside.

Butterfly chicken breasts and pound with chef's mallet to uniform thickness. Place one-quarter of the salmon mixture on each breast; fold into package, pressing edges to adhere.

Keeping remaining phyllo covered to prevent drying out, place 1 phyllo sheet on work surface; brush with butter. Place second sheet on top and brush with butter. Place 1 chicken breast on 1 short edge of phyllo; wrap phyllo around breast, folding in sides to form neat package. Brush with butter and place on baking sheet. Repeat with remaining phyllo, butter and breasts. Bake in 375°F oven for about 18 minutes or until firm to the touch and phyllo is golden.

TO SERVE: Arrange phyllo-wrapped breasts on warmed plates (whole or sliced on the diagonal). Drizzle with warm Sour Cherry Glaze. *Serves 4.*

1/2	lb sour cherries, pitted
1	tbsp orange zest
1	cup orange juice
1/2	cup water
1	tbsp granulated sugar
1	tsp grated gingerroot
	lemon juice (optional)*

Sour Cherry Ginger Glaze

In saucepan, bring cherries, orange zest and juice, water, sugar, gingerroot, and lemon juice (if using) to boil; cook, stirring, until reduced to desired consistency. *Makes about 1 cup.*

*If using sweeter fruit for glaze, you may want to add lemon juice to increase tartness.

Wine steward Ross Cave's wine suggestion: Gray Monk Pinot Gris

CRANBERRY-STUFFED PORK TENDERLOIN IN PHYLLO

THE OLD HOUSE RESTAURANT, COURTENAY, BC / *Chef: Trevor Schneider*

Pork tenderloin is one of the easiest cuts of meat to prepare and serve. It is low in fat, exceptionally tender and lends itself to a variety of preparations. This variation, featuring a creamy cranberry filling encrusted in crispy phyllo, makes a fine dinner presentation. Accompany with vegetables of choice.

1	pork tenderloin, 1 1/2 lb
2	tbsp olive oil
3/4	cup cream cheese, at room temperature
1/2	cup dried cranberries, coarsely chopped
1/4	tsp salt
1/4	tsp pepper
1/4	tsp cayenne pepper
8	sheets phyllo pastry
1/2	cup butter, melted

Trim fat from tenderloin. In heavy-based skillet, heat oil over medium-high heat; sear tenderloins on all sides. Transfer to plate and let cool to room temperature.

Meanwhile, in bowl, mix together cream cheese, cranberries, salt, pepper and cayenne pepper until smooth; set aside.

Cut tenderloin in 4 equal portions. Lay 1 sheet of phyllo on work surface, keeping remainder covered to prevent drying out; brush lightly with butter. Lay second sheet on top and brush with butter. Centre 1 piece of tenderloin at short edge of phyllo; spread with 1/4 of the cranberry mixture. Roll up phyllo around tenderloin to make neat package, stopping halfway to tuck in sides. Brush with butter. Repeat with remaining phyllo, butter and tenderloins.

Place packages on ungreased baking sheet; bake in 350°F oven for 15 to 20 minutes or until phyllo is browned and just a hint of pink remains inside pork. (Watch carefully as phyllo burns easily.)

TO SERVE: Carefully cut tenderloin crosswise into 1/2 inch thick slices and arrange on warmed plates. *Serves 4.*

VEAL WITH LEMON CAPER SAUCE

BORGO ANTICO RISTORANTE, VANCOUVER, BC / *Owner: Umberto Menghi*

Veal traditionally marries well with lemon and this recipe is no exception: succulent, tender veal simmers in a creamy lemon caper sauce. Medallions of veal tenderloin are used for this recipe at Borgo Antico. For ease in purchasing we have used veal scaloppine with excellent results. Serve with steamed vegetables and roasted new potatoes.

1	lb veal scaloppine
	salt and pepper
1/2	cup all-purpose flour
1	tbsp olive oil
1/4	cup dry white wine
	juice of 1/2 large lemon
1	cup rich homemade chicken stock*
1	tbsp capers, drained

Season veal with salt and pepper; dredge in flour to coat. Heat large skillet over medium heat and drizzle with enough oil to lightly cover surface; sear veal briefly on each side. Transfer to plate and keep warm.

Deglaze pan with wine; stir in lemon juice. Add chicken stock and capers; cook until reduced slightly. Return veal to pan and cook for 3 to 5 minutes or until veal is medium. Transfer to warmed serving dish. Continue cooking sauce, stirring, until reduced to desired thickness.

TO SERVE: Pour sauce over veal. *Serves 4.*

*You can substitute 2 cups canned low-sodium chicken broth cooked until it is reduced by half.

Chef's wine suggestion: Cedar Creek Sauvignon Blanc VQA, 1997

EDGEWATER MARINATED VENISON MEDALLIONS

EDGEWATER LODGE, WHISTLER, BC / *Executive Chef: Thomas Piekarski*

Edgewater's venison is farm-raised on the lodge's own ranch — Ruddock's Gold Pan Ranch near Lillooet, about a two-hour drive north of Whistler. It is as fresh as can be and unbelievably succulent. Chef Thomas Piekarski serves this entrée with a shiitake, green peppercorn and cognac sauce or cranberry sauce. You can use the Spicy Cranberry Sauce on page 16.

1/2	cup vegetable oil
6	cloves garlic, quartered
2	tbsp dry red wine
1	tsp fresh chopped rosemary
1/2	tsp pepper
2	bay leaves
4	pieces fresh venison, each 3 to 5 oz
1	tsp olive oil
1 to 2	tbsp Dijon mustard
2	cloves garlic, minced

In bowl, whisk together vegetable oil, garlic, wine, rosemary, pepper and bay leaves.

Lightly pound venison with meat hammer against the grain until 1 inch thick. Add to bowl and marinate in refrigerator overnight.

Remove venison from marinade shaking off excess. In skillet, heat olive oil over high heat; pan-sear venison on both sides until desired rareness. Remove from heat; brush medallions with Dijon mustard and top with garlic. *Serves 4.*

HAY-ROASTED FRASER VALLEY POUSSINS WITH CREAMY PARMESAN POLENTA

THE WILDFLOWER RESTAURANT AT CP CHATEAU WHISTLER RESORT / *Executive Chef: Glenn Monk*

From the kitchen at Chateau Whistler Resort comes this novel poultry dish featuring individual young chickens roasted on fresh hay. (Ensure that the hay you use is pesticide-free.) The restaurant makes a special effort to use local ingredients and obtains succulent young poultry from producers in the Fraser Valley, southeast of Vancouver. If unable to find young chickens (poussins), substitute Cornish hens. Serve seasonal vegetables alongside.

1	lb fresh dry hay
6	poussins (or 6 small Cornish hens)
	salt and pepper
	assorted sprigs fresh herbs (thyme, basil, rosemary, marjoram, etc.)
1	apple or pear, peeled and cut in small wedges
1	tbsp extra-virgin olive oil (approx)
1	bulb garlic
	Creamy Parmesan Polenta (recipe follows)

Soak hay in water for 5 minutes; drain and spread in bottom of large roasting pan.

Season poussins inside and out with salt and pepper. Fill cavities with a few of the herb sprigs and apple wedges; brush birds with some of the oil. Arrange birds on hay, leaving space between them.

Remove loose skin from garlic bulb; snip top of bulb to expose ends of individual cloves and rub entire surface with olive oil. Separate individual cloves and place around birds along with remaining herbs. Bake in 425°F oven for 25 to 35 minutes or until juices run clear when birds are pierced. Remove from oven and let stand for 10 minutes; remove any hay that is stuck to birds.

TO SERVE: Present poussins "family-style" on large platter with herbs and roasted garlic. (or remove breast meat from bone) and remove legs and thighs; divide among warmed dinner plates along with herbs and garlic.) Accompany with Creamy Parmesan Polenta. *Serves 6.*

4	cups vegetable stock (or water)
1	cup yellow cornmeal
1/3	cup butter
1 1/3	cups grated Parmesan cheese
	salt and white pepper

Creamy Parmesan Polenta

In saucepan, bring vegetable stock to boil. Gradually stir in cornmeal, whisking constantly; reduce heat and simmer for 15 minutes, stirring occasionally.

Gradually add butter and Parmesan, stirring until blended. Season with salt and pepper to taste. Pour into individual buttered ramekins or medium casserole dish. Let stand for 10 to 15 minutes or until polenta is firmly moulded. Invert onto dinner plates or large serving dish. *Serves 6.*

BRAISED RABBIT WITH WILD MUSHROOMS, FRESH HERBS AND MASCARPONE POLENTA

THE MAHLE HOUSE RESTAURANT, NANAIMO, BC / *Owner/Chef: Maureen Loucks*

At the Mahle House Restaurant the chef uses front and back legs from 3 rabbits in this recipe, reserving the loins to grill with a Dijon mustard sauce. For the home kitchen we have adjusted the recipe to use 1 to 2 rabbits. If using rabbit stock prepare it one day in advance to allow flavours to blend.

1 or 2	rabbits (3 to 4 lb total)
2	tbsp unsalted butter
2	tbsp olive oil
1	large onion, diced
3 to 4	cloves garlic, minced
12	oz fresh chanterelle mushrooms, sliced (or mushrooms of choice, sliced)
3	cups Rabbit Stock (recipe follows)*
3	tbsp chopped fresh rosemary, thyme and sage
	salt and pepper
	Mascarpone Polenta (recipe follows)

Remove loins and front and back legs from rabbit(s); reserve remainder for stock.

In skillet, heat butter and oil over medium-low heat: sauté rabbit pieces for 4 to 5 minutes, stirring, until golden brown. Transfer to large baking pan. In same skillet and adding more butter and oil if necessary, sauté onion, garlic and mushrooms, stirring often, for 5 minutes or until softened and browned. Pour in Rabbit Stock and cook until reduced slightly; stir in rosemary, thyme and sage. Season with salt and pepper to taste.

Pour mushroom mixture over rabbit; cover pan with foil and bake in 375°F oven for 1 hour or until well braised. Transfer rabbit to plate and keep warm. Pour braising liquid into saucepan; bring to boil and reduce, stirring, until sauce is thickened.

TO SERVE: Arrange rabbit on warmed plates, top with sauce, and accompany with Mascarpone Polenta alongside. *Serves 4.*

Chicken stock or mild beef stock may be substituted for rabbit stock.

2	quarts water
	reserved rabbit
2	onions, chopped
2	carrots, chopped
1	stalk celery, sliced
3	cloves garlic, minced
1/2	tsp salt
1/2	tsp pepper

Rabbit Stock

In large saucepan, combine water, rabbit, onions, carrot, celery, garlic, salt and pepper; bring to boil. Reduce heat to simmer and cook, stirring occasionally, until reduced by half. Strain stock; adjust seasoning if necessary and set aside in refrigerator. Extra stock may be frozen for later use. *Makes 1 quart.*

Mascarpone Polenta

2	cups water
2	cups whole milk
1	cup yellow cornmeal
2	oz mascarpone cheese
1/4 to 1/2 cup 35% cream	
	salt and white pepper

In saucepan, bring water and milk to boil. Gradually stir in cornmeal, whisking constantly; reduce heat and simmer for 15 minutes, stirring occasionally. Stir in cheese and enough cream to make smooth texture. Season with salt and pepper to taste.

Pour into individual buttered ramekins or medium casserole dish. Let stand for 10 to 15 minutes or until polenta is firmly moulded. Invert onto dinner plates or large serving dish. *Serves 4 to 6.*

Owner Delbert Horrocks' wine suggestion: Alderlea Pinot Noir (Vancouver Island)

SEAFOOD ENTRÉES

LUCKY ARE THE RESIDENTS OF AN AREA WITH A LONG OCEAN COASTLINE FOR THEY ARE ABLE TO REAP THE FRESH BOUNTY the sea has to offer.

The chefs featured in this book delight in creating innovative seafood dishes with traditional and not-so-traditional ingredients and they generously share some of their finer recipes with us. Whether you prefer your seafood grilled, baked, smoked, sautéed, poached or even raw, you will find a recipe in this collection to tempt your palate. Seafood is often the easiest and quickest of entrées to prepare. For Grilled Fillet of Wild Salmon with Summer Salsa from The Latch Country Inn and Halibut Poêle with Lemon Potatoes and Hollandaise Sauce from La Rua Restaurante, it takes only a few minutes to cook the fish and just slightly longer for the sauces and vegetables.

A number of recipes reveal the Asian influence in Pacific Northwest cuisine: Pan-Charred Rare Tuna with Grotto-Style Sesame Sauce from The Grotto and Good Night Salmon from Tojo's Restaurant are delicious and well worth trying. Many of the recipes, such as Brioche and 7 C's Spice–Crusted Pacific Lingcod and Smoked Black Alaska Cod with Grainy Mustard Dill Beurre Blanc, include seasonings and sauces that are interchangeable and work well with a variety of seafood and meats.

◄ Halibut Poêle with Lemon Potatoes and Chive Butter Sauce

HALIBUT POÊLE WITH LEMON POTATOES AND CHIVE BUTTER SAUCE

LA RUA RESTAURANTE, WHISTLER, BC / *Executive Chef: Tim Muehlbauer*

Halibut marries well with citrus flavours, and Tim Muehlbauer's accompaniment of citrus-flavoured Yukon gold potatoes provides a unique accent. Serve seared Roma tomatoes and steamed asparagus alongside.

1 1/2 to 2 lb halibut fillets each 6 oz
1   cup fish stock
2   tbsp butter
Lemon Potatoes (recipe follows)
Chive Butter Sauce (recipe follows)

On grill over high heat, briefly sear fish to mark. Transfer to baking dish; pour in stock and dot fish with butter. Bake in 350°F oven for 10 minutes or until fish is opaque and flakes easily. Set aside and keep warm. Drain stock into small saucepan over medium heat; cook, stirring often, until reduced by half.

TO SERVE: Arrange Lemon Potatoes in centre of plates. Drizzle Chive Butter Sauce around potatoes and sprinkle with chives. Place fish on top of potatoes and drizzle with reduced stock. *Serves 4 to 6.*

2   lb Yukon gold potatoes, peeled and cut in 1/2-inch cubes
zest and juice of 1 each lime, lemon and orange

Lemon Potatoes

In saucepan, combine potatoes and lime, lemon and orange zest and juice. Pour in enough water to cover potatoes; bring to boil. Reduce heat and simmer for 8 to 10 minutes or until potatoes are cooked but still firm. Remove from heat and let stand in cooking water for 30 minutes. Drain and serve. *Makes 5 to 6 cups.*

1/2 cup unsalted butter
2   tsp lemon juice
2   tbsp chopped chives

Chive Butter Sauce

In small saucepan, heat butter over low heat stirring frequently, until it turns light golden and gives off a nutty fragrance. Carefully stir lemon juice into butter; stir in chives. *Makes 1/2 cup.*

1912 SCALLOP AND PRAWN SAUTÉ

THE HISTORIC 1912 RESTAURANT AND COUNTRY INN, KALEDEN, BC / *Owners: Donna and Allan Dell*

The Dells take full advantage of the fresh produce grown in the Okanagan Valley and change their recipes to accommodate what is in season. If pears are not "ripe from the tree," they recommend substituting the freshest fruit you can find.

2	tsp extra-virgin olive oil
1	lb jumbo prawns, peeled and deveined
1	lb large sea scallops
2	tbsp cold butter
2	tsp minced garlic
2	green onions, julienned
1	cup julienned leek (white part only)
2	Bartlett pears, peeled and sliced
1/2	cup Sumac Ridge Gewürztraminer (or other sweet white wine)
2	tbsp lemon juice
	pinch each dried basil, tarragon, oregano and thyme
	salt and pepper
4 to 5	cups cooked basmati rice or other long-grain rice

In large skillet, heat oil over medium-high heat; sear scallops and prawns. Transfer to plate and keep warm. Add half of the butter, garlic, onions, leek and pears; sauté, stirring, for 3 to 4 minutes or until slightly softened. Return seafood to pan and deglaze with wine and lemon juice. Add basil, tarragon, oregano and thyme and bring to boil; stir remaining butter into sauce to thicken. Season with salt and pepper to taste.

TO SERVE: Spoon seafood over rice. *Serves 4 to 6.*

Chef's wine suggestion: Sumac Ridge Gewürztraminer

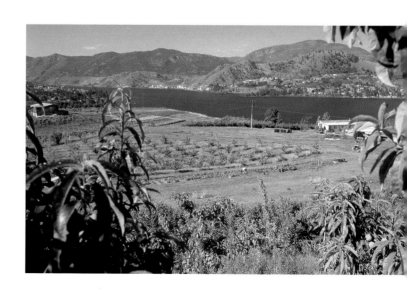

SCALLOPS NAPOLEON

THE MAHLE HOUSE RESTAURANT, NANAIMO, BC / *Owner/Chef: Maureen Loucks*

Chef Maureen Loucks loves to create from basics, using fresh local ingredients to full advantage. The restaurant's own organic kitchen garden supplies her with an incredible variety of gourmet vegetables. This seafood entrée has great visual appeal and will delight your palate with its contrasting textures and flavours. Make Lemon Oil one week in advance or use commercially prepared lemon oil.

1 to 2	yams, enough for 12 1/4-inch thick slices (or sweet potato)
1	tbsp unsalted butter
1	tbsp olive oil
1 1/2 lb	large scallops (10 to 20 count)
	Sherried Shiitake and Brown Mushroom Confit (recipe follows)
	Lemon Oil (recipe follows)

Prick yams with fork; microwave at high for 6 to 8 minutes until almost cooked. Let cool. Carefully peel yams and slice each into 12 rounds each about 1/4 inch thick. Transfer to grill over medium heat and cook for 2 to 4 minutes or until tender and slightly browned. (Or in lightly greased skillet over medium heat, sauté slices for 2 to 4 minutes or until browned.) Set aside and keep warm.

In large skillet, heat butter and olive oil over medium-high heat: sauté scallops for 8 to 10 minutes or until opaque, being careful not to overcook.

TO SERVE: Place yam slice in centre of each plate. Top with 1 tbsp Sherried Shiitake and Brown Mushroom Confit. Place 2 or 3 scallops on confit and top with another yam slice. Drizzle Lemon Oil around scallops. *Serves 4 to 6.*

1 1/2	tsp olive oil
1	tsp butter
3	shallots, minced
1/2	lb cremini mushrooms (or cultivated white mushrooms) chopped
1/4	lb shiitake mushrooms, chopped
1/2	cup chicken stock
2	tbsp medium dry sherry
	salt and pepper

Sherried Shiitake and Brown Mushroom Confit

In skillet, heat oil and butter over medium-low heat; sweat shallots until softened. Raise heat to medium. Add cremini and shiitake mushrooms; cook, stirring often, for 4 to 6 minutes or until softened. Add stock and simmer, stirring, for 5 to 6 minutes or until thick and rich. Stir in sherry, and salt and pepper to taste. *Makes 2 cups.*

1 cup vegetable oil
2 tbsp olive oil
  zest and juice of 3 lemons
  pinch turmeric (optional)

Lemon Oil

Use lemon-flavoured oil in salads and to sauté chicken or fish.

In blender, combine vegetable and olive oils, lemon zest and juice and turmeric; process until blended. Funnel into bottle and store in refrigerator for 1 week to infuse flavours. Let come to room temperature. (At this point the oil will separate.) Carefully remove oil from liquid, discarding liquid. Strain oil through fine sieve; return to bottle and refrigerate. *Makes 1 cup.*

Owner Delbert Horrocks' wine suggestion: Fetzer Bonterra Chardonnay

AL GRANCHIO (BLACK SQUID PASTA WITH DUNGENESS CRAB SAUCE)

QUATTRO AT WHISTLER, WHISTLER, BC / *Executive Chef/Manager: Rob Parrott*

This entrée makes a very dramatic presentation with its fresh black squid-ink pasta topped with a delicate slightly pink sauce. Try to locate fresh squid-ink fettuccine; if unable, substitute regular semolina fettuccine.

1	tbsp butter
1/4	up finely diced onion
1	tbsp minced garlic
1/2	lb fresh Dungeness crabmeat
1/4	cup brandy
1	cup 35% cream
1/2	cup tomato sauce
1/3	cup chopped fresh basil
	pinch red pepper flakes
	salt
1	lb fresh squid-ink fettuccine

In heavy-based skillet heat butter over medium heat; sauté onion and garlic, stirring often, until softened but not browned. Add crabmeat and sauté until heated through. Pour in brandy and flambé, stirring, until all flames subside. Add cream, tomato sauce, basil and red pepper flakes; simmer for about 5 minutes or until reduced slightly. Season with salt to taste.

Meanwhile, cook fettuccine according to package directions until al dente.

TO SERVE: Divide fettuccine among warmed plates and top with sauce. Garnish with basil. *Serves 4.*

SEARED MEDALLION OF SMOKED ALASKAN BLACK COD WITH POTATO ARTICHOKE HASH AND SCALLION OIL

DIVA AT THE MET, VANCOUVER, BC / *Executive Chef: Michael Noble*

Chef Michael Noble has created an updated version of the traditional smoked cod fish and potato dinner: cook the cod to perfection, dress it with a unique potato and artichoke hash, and drizzle with Scallion Oil.

When purchasing, look for "natural smoked cod" which is not over-salted. If the cod is too salty, place in bowl and pour enough milk over fish just to cover. Refrigerate 4 to 8 hours to leach out excess salt; drain and pat dry.

4	smoked Alaska black cod fillets, each 6 oz (optional Atlantic smoked cod)
1	tbsp olive oil
2	tsp butter
	pepper
	Potato Artichoke Hash (recipe follows)
	Scallion Oil (recipe follows)

In skillet, heat oil and butter over medium-high heat; sauté fish until opaque and slightly caramelized. Season with pepper to taste.

TO SERVE: Divide Potato Artichoke Hash among plates, top with fish and drizzle with Scallion Oil. *Serves 4.*

Potato Artichoke Hash

1 1/2	lb baking potatoes, peeled and diced
3	tbsp unsalted butter
1/2	cup finely diced red onion
1	sweet red pepper, finely diced
4	fresh artichoke bottoms, trimmed, poached and diced (or 4 canned, diced)
2	cloves garlic, minced
1	tbsp chopped fresh chervil (or 1 tsp dried)
1	tbsp chopped fresh parsley (or 1 tsp dried)
	salt and white pepper

In saucepan, blanch potatoes in boiling water until tender. Drain well. In skillet, heat butter over medium heat; sauté diced potato until slightly browned; add onion and red pepper and additional butter if necessary; cook for 2 to 3 minutes or until golden. Near end of cooking add artichokes, garlic, parsley, chervil and salt and pepper to taste. *Makes 4 to 5 cups.*

Scallion Oil

4	green onions (green part only), coarsely chopped
1/2	cup extra-virgin olive oil
	pinch ground white pepper

In bowl, stir together green onions, oil and pepper; refrigerate for at least 2 hours or for up to 5 hours. Transfer to blender and purée. Taste and adjust seasoning if necessary. *Makes 1/2 cup.*

GRILLED HALIBUT T-BONE WITH SUMMER VEGETABLE SALAD AND CRÈME FRAÎCHE MOUSSE

THE AERIE RESORT, MALAHAT, BC / *Chef de Cuisine: Chris Jones*

Chef de cuisine Chris Jones insists that only the freshest of local produce and seafood be served from the kitchen at The Aerie. In this entrée, he features mild-flavoured Pacific halibut accompanied by a salad of fennel-flavoured local baby vegetables.

2	halibut steaks, each 1 lb
1	tbsp olive oil
1	cup crème fraîche*, whipped
2	tbsp fresh fennel buds (optional)
	Summer Vegetable Salad (recipe follows)
	olive oil (cold-pressed or extra virgin)
	salt and cracked black pepper
4	sprigs each fresh tarragon and fennel frond

Preheat one side of grill to high. Cut halibut steaks in half through centre bone. Brush fish with oil and grill for 2 to 3 minutes per side. Transfer to unheated side of grill; close lid and cook for 2 to 3 minutes longer. Transfer to plate and keep warm.

If using fennel buds, fold into whipped crème fraîche.

TO SERVE: Arrange Summer Vegetable Salad in centre of plates, top with fish and spoon dollop of crème fraîche on fish. Drizzle oil around salad; season with salt and pepper to taste, and garnish with tarragon and fennel fronds. *Serves 4.*

*Traditional crème fraîche is sold in some specialty markets but is also easy to duplicate at home. In a glass bowl, stir together 1 cup 35% cream and 2 tbsp buttermilk. Cover and let stand at room temperature for at least 8 or up to 24 hours. When thick, stir, cover and refrigerate for up to 10 days.

2	cups shaved fennel bulb
1 1/2	cups yellow baby beets, blanched and thinly sliced
1 1/2	cups new potatoes, cooked and thinly sliced
1	tbsp olive oil
	salt and pepper

Summer Vegetable Salad

In bowl, combine shaved fennel, baby beets and potatoes; toss with oil until just coated. Season with salt and pepper to taste. *Makes 5 cups.*

COCONUT MILK AND MASALA MUSSELS

BIN 941 TAPAS PARLOUR, VANCOUVER, BC / *Owner/Chef: Gord Martin*

At BIN 941 fresh mussels are prepared in four ways, each highlighting the cuisine of a distinct region. From the menu, chef Martin chose this slightly sweet and aromatic Thai variation for you to re-create at home. Accompany the mussels with warm focaccia or other bread.

3 to 4	lb mussels
3	tbsp extra-virgin olive oil
1	large leek (white part only), julienned
1	cup canned coconut milk
3/4	cup dry white wine
1	tbsp lemon zest (thinly grated)
1/2	tsp garam masala*
	pinch red pepper flakes

Scrub mussels and remove beards. Discard any that have broken shells or that do not close when tapped. In a large saucepan, heat oil over medium heat; sauté leeks briefly. Stir in coconut milk, wine, lemon zest, garam masala and red pepper flakes; bring to a boil. Add mussels, cover and steam for 3 to 5 minutes or until mussels are opened. (Discard any that have not opened.)

TO SERVE: Arrange mussels in individual bowls and pour sauce over top. *Serves 4 as main course or 6 as an appetizer.*

*Garam masala is a traditional Indian seasoning of dry-roasted ground spices from the northern regions of the country. It is available in the gourmet section of some supermarkets or at Indian markets.

BRANZIO ALLA CROSTA (CRUSTED SEA BASS)

QUATTRO AT WHISTLER, WHISTLER, BC / *Executive Chef/Manager: Rob Parrott*

This recipe is probably the most popular entrée at Quattro at Whistler. Though the restaurant's menu changes quarterly, this dish has remained the top seller during the past three years. Halibut, haddock or any other firm white fish works equally well in this recipe.

1 1/2	lb sea bass piece, skin removed
3	tbsp olive oil
2	cloves garlic, crushed
	salt and pepper
1	cup pistachio nuts, ground
	Roasted Sweet Pepper Sauce (recipe follows)

Cut fish into 4 portions. Whisk together oil, garlic, salt and pepper; brush over fish. Dredge fish in ground pistachios, pressing to adhere. Place in ovenproof skillet and bake in 400°F oven for 10 minutes or until fish is opaque and flakes easily.

TO SERVE: Place fish on warmed plates, drizzle with Roasted Sweet Pepper Sauce and accompany with vegetables of choice. *Serves 4.*

1	sweet red pepper
1	sweet yellow pepper
1/4	cup chopped fresh basil
1	tsp minced garlic
1/4	cup fish stock
1/4	cup 35% cream
	salt and pepper

Roasted Sweet Pepper Sauce

On baking sheet, roast red and yellow peppers in 425°F oven for 15 minutes or until skins begin to wrinkle and bracken. Transfer to bowl, cover with plastic wrap and set aside for 30 minutes.

Peel peppers and remove membranes and seeds; in food processor, purée until smooth. Add basil, garlic, fish stock and cream; purée until blended. Season with salt and pepper to taste. Transfer sauce to small saucepan and simmer over medium heat, stirring often, for 10 minutes or until slightly thickened. *Makes 2 cups.*

ALMOND GINGER–CRUSTED CHILEAN SEA BASS WITH ORANGE LIME BEURRE BLANC

RIM ROCK CAFÉ, WHISTLER, BC / *Owner/Chef: Rolf Gunther*

The firm yet moist texture of this ocean fish, lightly crusted with a nutty ginger batter and drizzled with orange lime butter sauce, garners rave reviews.

4 to 6	sea bass fillets, each 6 oz
	salt and pepper
1	tbsp lemon juice
1/2	cup almonds, chopped
1	tbsp cornstarch
1	tbsp minced shallots
1	tbsp grated gingerroot
1	egg white
1/4	cup sake (Japanese wine)
1 1/2	tbsp vegetable oil
1 1/2	tbsp butter
	Orange Lime Beurre Blanc (recipe follows)
	thin slices orange and lime

Season sea bass with salt and pepper and drizzle with lemon juice. In bowl, combine almonds, cornstarch, shallots and gingerroot. Whisk egg white with sake until frothy; stir in almond mixture until combined. Dip 1 side of each fillet into batter, coating well.

In heavy-based skillet, heat oil and butter over medium-high heat; fry fish, batter side down for 5 minutes until golden brown. Carefully turn over and cook until fish is opaque and flakes easily.

TO SERVE: Place fish, crust side up, on warmed plates; drizzle with Orange Lime Beurre Blanc and garnish with orange and lime slices. *Serves 4 to 6.*

Orange Lime Beurre Blanc

3/4	cup orange juice
1/3	cup lime juice
3	tbsp 35% cream, whipped
1/2	cup cold butter, cubed

In small saucepan over medium heat, stir together orange and lime juices; cook, stirring occasionally, for about 15 minutes or until reduced to syrupy consistency. Add whipped cream and cook for about 5 minutes or until reduced by half. Whisk in butter, 1 cube at a time, until melted and sauce is creamy. Keep warm until serving. *Makes 1 cup.*

PAN-CHARRED RARE TUNA WITH GROTTO-STYLE SESAME SAUCE

THE GROTTO, NANAIMO, BC / *Owner: Mike Yoshida, Chef: Dave Armour*

The secret to a succulent tuna dish is to purchase the fish as fresh and as thick as possible, then cook it over very high heat to rare or medium rare, ensuring that moisture is retained.

1 1/2	lb tuna piece, (approx 1 inch thick)
1/2	head Boston or Bibb lettuce
1	green onion, chopped
	Grotto-Style Sesame Sauce (recipe follows)

On barbecue or grill over high heat, cook fish, turning once, for 3 to 5 minutes for rare, or 5 to 7 minutes for medium-rare. Slice thinly.

TO SERVE: Arrange lettuce on large plates. Fan tuna slices over top and drizzle with Grotto-Style Sesame Sauce. *Serves 4.*

2	tbsp sesame seeds, toasted*
1/4	cup light soy sauce
3	tbsp mirin (Japanese rice wine)
1 1/2	tsp wasabi powder (or 1/2 tsp wasabi paste)
	pinch dashi**

Grotto-Style Sesame sauce

With mortar and pestle, lightly crush sesame seeds. In food processor, combine crushed sesame seeds, soy sauce, mirin, wasabi powder and dashi; process until consistency of sauce. Cover and refrigerate until serving. *Makes 1/2 cup.*

Toast sesame seeds in dry skillet over medium heat, shaking gently, for 3 to 4 minutes until golden.

**Japanese dried fish–based soup stock*

Wine suggestion: Grey Monk's 97 Pinot Gris or other crisp, full-bodied dry white

SOOKE HARBOUR HOUSE STEAMED SKATE WING WITH CRANBERRY VINEGAR SAUCE

SOOKE HARBOUR HOUSE, SOOKE, BC / *Luncheon Chef: Pia Carroll*

The chefs at Sooke Harbour House revel in experimentation and love to weave unusual ingredients into their recipes. Skate, also known as ray, are kite-shaped bottom-feeding fish with edible, wing-like pectoral fins. The flesh is sweet with a texture not unlike scallops. If unable to obtain skate wing, you may want to serve the Cranberry Vinegar Sauce with poached halibut or salmon.

1 1/2	lb skate wing, skin and bone removed
	Cranberry Vinegar Sauce (recipe follows)

Divide skate into 4 6-oz portions. In steamer or large saucepan with steaming basket, bring small amount of water to boil over medium-high heat; add skate, cover and cook for 4 to 5 minutes or until opaque throughout. Remove with slotted spatula and let drain on paper towel.

TO SERVE: Pour Cranberry Vinegar Sauce on warmed plates and place skate wings on top. *Serves 4.*

Cranberry Vinegar Sauce

1	cup fish stock
1/2	cup dry white wine
1	clove garlic, minced
1	shallot, minced
1/3	cup Cranberry Vinegar (recipe follows)
1/3	cup unsalted butter

In heavy-based saucepan, bring fish stock, wine, garlic and shallot to boil over high heat; cook, stirring often, until reduced to syrupy consistency. Add Cranberry Vinegar and cook for 1 minute. Remove from heat and gradually whisk in butter. Set aside and keep warm. *Makes 3/4 cup.*

Cranberry Vinegar

1	cup fresh or frozen cranberries
1/2	cup white wine vinegar or pure apple cider vinegar

This flavoured vinegar is great to have on hand for salad dressings or to accompany fish dishes in lieu of lemon wedges. For a larger yield, simply increase the amount of cranberries and vinegar proportionately. Make it at least one day in advance to allow flavours to blend.

In saucepan, bruise cranberries with wooden spoon, being careful not to mash. Pour in vinegar; bring to boil, stirring, over high heat. Remove from heat and let stand 10 minutes.

Pour vinegar through fine-mesh sieve into bowl. When cool, funnel into sterilized bottles and seal. Store in cool, dark place.

SMOKED BLACK ALASKA COD WITH GRAINY MUSTARD DILL BEURRE BLANC

SEASONS RESTAURANT IN QUEEN ELIZABETH PARK, VANCOUVER, BC / *Executive Chef: Pierre Delacote*

Black Alaskan cod, also referred to as butterfish and sablefish, lends itself well to smoking. Chef Delacote suggests serving potatoes mashed with garlic and olive oil with this rustic dish.

4 to 6	boneless skinless smoked Alaskan black cod fillets*, each 6 oz (optional Atlantic smoked cod)
	milk
	Grainy Mustard Dill Beurre Blanc (recipe follows)
	thinly sliced red onion rings
2	tbsp capers, drained
	fresh dill sprigs

In shallow pan, pour enough milk over fish just to cover; bring to boil. Reduce heat to medium-low, cover and simmer for 8 to 10 minutes or until opaque. Drain and remove any milk residue from fillets.

TO SERVE: Place fillets on warmed plates; coat with Grainy Mustard Beurre Blanc and top with onion rings, capers and dill sprigs. Accompany with vegetables of choice. *Serves 4 to 6.*

*Some varieties of smoked cod are very salty. To reduce saltiness, place cod in bowl, cover with milk and refrigerate for 4 to 8 hours. Drain and proceed with recipe.

1	cup dry white wine
1/2	cup white wine vinegar
1/4	cup minced shallots
3/4	cup chilled unsalted butter, cubed
2	tbsp grainy Dijon mustard
2	tsp hot Dijon mustard
1	tbsp chopped fresh dill (or 1 tsp dried dillweed)
1	tsp liquid honey
	salt and pepper

Grainy Mustard Dill Beurre Blanc

In small saucepan, stir together wine, vinegar and shallots; bring to boil and cook, stirring often, until reduced by one-third. Reduce heat to low to keep sauce hot without simmering. Whisking constantly, add cubes of butter 1 at a time, stirring until melted and sauce is light and creamy. Whisk in grainy and hot Dijon mustards, dill, honey, and salt and pepper to taste. *Makes 1 1/2 cups.*

CEDAR-INFUSED B.C. SALMON WITH ONION CONFIT AND HAZELNUT AND BALSAMIC VINAIGRETTE

VAL D'ISÈRE RESTAURANT, WHISTLER, BC / *Owner/Chef: Roland Pfaff*

Part of the delight of this dish is the aroma that wafts through your kitchen from the baking cedar plank. Roland Pfaff serves his delicately flavoured salmon entrée over a scattering of sautéed sea asparagus accompanied by colourful Sun-Dried Tomato Risotto (see page 108). Sea asparagus grows in the cold waters of the North Pacific and can be purchased in specialty markets throughout the Pacific Northwest.

1	untreated cedar plank*
1 1/2	lb salmon fillets (with skin), 6-oz portions
1	tsp olive oil
	Onion Confit (recipe follows)
	Sautéed Sea Asparagus (recipe follows)
	Hazelnut Vinaigrette (recipe follows)
1/3	cup chopped toasted hazelnuts
	fresh herbs

Soak cedar plank in water for 4 to 6 hours. Lightly brush skin side of salmon with oil. Heat grill to high; briefly sear skin side of fish to mark. Place fish, skin side down, on cedar plank and bake in 375°F oven for 8 to 10 minutes. Top fish with Onion Confit; bake for 1 minute or until fish is medium-rare. Gently slide knife between salmon and skin to separate.

TO SERVE: Centre skin, crunchy side up on plates; scatter sea asparagus over plate. Cut fish portions into 3 or 4 medallions and arrange over skin. Drizzle with Hazelnut Vinaigrette, sprinkle with toasted hazelnuts and garnish with fresh herbs. *Serves 4.*

Look for an untreated cedar fence board at hardware stores or in lumber yards and ask to have it cut to desired lengths.

Onion Confit

2/3	cup water
2	tbsp red wine vinegar
1	sweet onion, chopped
	dash grenadine (or drop red food colouring)

In saucepan over medium-low heat, stir together water, wine, onion and grenadine; simmer for about 20 minutes or until onions are very tender. Set aside. *Makes 1 cup.*

Sautéed Sea Asparagus

	small bunch sea asparagus
1	tsp olive oil

In pot of boiling water, blanch asparagus; drain and pat dry. In skillet, heat oil over medium heat; sauté asparagus, stirring often, until barely tender. Set aside. *Makes 1 cup.*

4	tbsp hazelnut oil
2	tbsp balsamic vinegar
2	tbsp fish stock

Hazelnut Vinaigrette

In blender, mix together oil, vinegar and fish stock. Set aside.
Makes 1/2 cup.

CIN CIN POACHED SALMON WITH SORREL SAUCE

CIN CIN, VANCOUVER, BC / *Executive Chef: Romy Prasad*

Salmon is probably the best-known variety of fish in the Pacific Northwest, and every restaurant has its own special preparation. This delicate poached version from the kitchen of Romy Prasad is easy to prepare and tastes wonderful.

6	cups water
1	cup dry white wine
1/2	stalk celery, sliced
1/2	carrot, sliced
1/4	cup diced onion
1	small lemon, thinly sliced
1	tsp salt
1	tsp coriander seeds
5	sprigs fresh cilantro
5	sprigs fresh parsley
3	sprigs fresh thyme
5	sprigs fresh dill
1/2	cup white wine vinegar
4	salmon fillets, each 6 oz
	Asparagus, Sweet Pepper and Tomato Salad (recipe follows)
	Sorrel Sauce (recipe follows)

In large saucepan, combine water, wine, celery, carrot, onion, lemon slices, salt, coriander seeds, fresh cilantro, parsley, thyme and dill; bring to boil. Reduce heat and simmer for 10 minutes. Add vinegar and simmer for 5 minutes longer. Gently place fish in bouillon; return to simmer, cover and poach for 8 to 10 minutes or until opaque.

TO SERVE: Divide salad among plates; with slotted spoon, transfer fish to top of salad and top with Sorrel Sauce. *Serves 4.*

1	tomato, seeded and diced
1/2	sweet red pepper, diced
1/2	sweet green pepper, diced
4	asparagus spears (tender part only), thinly sliced
1	small bunch watercress

Asparagus, Sweet Pepper and Tomato Salad

In bowl, combine tomato, red and green peppers, asparagus and watercress. Set aside until serving. *Makes 3 to 4 cups.*

Sorrel Sauce

If fresh sorrel is unavailable you may substitute watercress, but the flavour will be more subtle.

1   egg
2   cups fresh sorrel
1/2   tsp vinegar
     generous dash Tabasco Sauce
1/4   cup grapeseed oil
     salt and pepper

In food processor, combine egg, sorrel, vinegar and Tabasco: process until smooth. With machine running, add oil in slow steady stream, processing until slightly thickened. Cover and refrigerate; remove from refrigerator 10 minutes before serving to let come to room temperature. Taste and adjust seasoning with salt and pepper if necessary. *Makes 3/4 cup.*

GRILLED FILLET OF WILD SALMON WITH SUMMER SALSA

THE LATCH COUNTRY INN, SIDNEY, BC / *Innkeeper: Heidi Rust*

The kitchen at The Latch Country Inn specializes in European cuisine highlighted with fresh British Columbia ingredients. The special emphasis on lighter, healthier fare is evident in the perfect balance of this salmon and fresh salsa entrée. Complete the course with roasted baby red-skinned potatoes and a medley of steamed vegetables. If you like a grilled appearance to your salmon, quickly sear fillets on grill for 1 minute before baking.

4	wild salmon fillets, each 5 oz
2	tbsp lemon juice
	salt and pepper
	Summer Salsa

Brush salmon with lemon juice and sprinkle with salt and pepper. Place in ovenproof dish and bake at 400°F for 6 to 8 minutes or until opaque and flakes easily.

TO SERVE: Place fish on warmed plates; spoon Summer Salsa alongside. *Serves 4.*

Summer Salsa

1/4	cup olive oil
1/4	cup minced shallots
1	tbsp lemon zest
2	tbsp lemon juice
12	oz cherry tomatoes, quartered
1/2	English cucumber, peeled and diced
1/4	cup red onion, diced
1/2	large yellow pepper, diced
2	tbsp capers, drained
1	tbsp cilantro, chopped

In small bowl, whisk together oil, shallots and lemon zest and juice until well blended. In large bowl, combine tomatoes, cucumber, onion, yellow pepper, capers and cilantro; pour dressing over top and stir to combine. *Makes 4 to 5 cups.*

Innkeeper's wine suggestion: Mission Hill Grand Reserve VQA Chardonnay

STILTON-CRUSTED SALMON FILLET WITH WARM CAPER RELISH AND SWEET SOY GLAZE

THE WESLEY STREET, NANAIMO, BC / *Executive Chef: Ian Ter Veer*

Topped with pungent Stilton cheese and a sweetened soy glaze, this is truly salmon with a difference. At The Wesley Street, it is served with creamy horseradish mashed potatoes.

4 sockeye salmon fillets, each 7 oz
salt and pepper
4 oz Stilton cheese
Sweet Soy Glaze (recipe follows)
Warm Caper Relish (recipe follows)

Season salmon with salt and pepper to taste. Crumble Stilton over each fillet, pressing lightly to adhere. Place fish on baking sheet and bake in 400°F oven for 5 to 10 minutes until medium-rare or desired doneness.

TO SERVE: Place fish on warmed plates, drizzle with Sweet Soy Glaze and garnish with Warm Caper Relish. *Serves 4.*

1 bunch green onions, chopped
1/2 small red onion, chopped
1 small sweet red pepper, diced
1/2 cup sweet white wine
zest and juice of 1 lime
3 tbsp liquid honey
1/4 cup capers, drained
1/4 cup ketjap manis*

Warm Caper Relish

In skillet over medium low heat, sauté onions and red pepper until tender-crisp. Transfer to bowl and set aside. Deglaze skillet with wine and lime juice and zest: cook, stirring often, until reduced by half. Add wine mixture to onion mixture along with honey, capers and ketjap manis; stir to combine. Keep warm until serving. *Makes 2/3 cup.*

1/4 cup ketjap manis*
1 tbsp wasabi powder
salt and pepper

Sweet Soy Glaze

In small saucepan, stir together ketjap manis, wasabi powder, and salt and pepper to taste; bring to gentle boil and cook, stirring, until reduced slightly. Remove from heat and keep warm until serving. *Makes 1/4 cup.*

*Ketjap manis, a thick, sweet Indonesian sauce, is available in Asian markets.

Chef's wine suggestion: British Columbia fruity Riesling of choice

WILD SALMON AND SORREL WITH FRESH GINGER JUICE SAUCE

HERALD STREET CAFFE, VICTORIA, BC / *Executive Chef: Mark Finnigan*

This creation from the kitchen of Mark Finnigan makes an impressive presentation. The salmon, sealed within its package of curly savoy cabbage, is cooked to perfection. Prepare Fresh Ginger Juice Sauce in advance.

1 1/3	lb salmon
8	sorrel leaves*
4	small sprigs fresh dill
1	head savoy cabbage
2	tbsp unsalted butter, melted
	salt and pepper
1/2	tsp cracked peppercorns
	Fresh Ginger Juice Sauce (recipe follows)
1	tbsp salmon roe or caviar

Cut salmon into 4 squares, each about 2 1/2" by 2 1/2". Place 2 sorrel leaves and 1 sprig dill on each. Set aside in refrigerator.

Discard outer leaves from cabbage; core and carefully remove 10 leaves. In large pot of boiling salted water, cook leaves for 6 to 8 minutes or until softened. Drain and refresh under cold running water; pat dry. Cut 8 of the best leaves into rectangles; brush with butter and season with salt and pepper to taste. Using 2 leaves, lay 1 over the other to form cross. Place salmon package in centre of cross and fold ends over; wrap tightly in plastic wrap and refrigerate. Repeat with remaining cabbage and salmon packages.

In large saucepan with steaming basket, bring small amount of water to simmer; arrange salmon packages in basket, cover and steam for 7 minutes. Remove saucepan from heat and let continue to cook for 3 to 4 minutes.

TO SERVE: Remove wrap from salmon and sprinkle with cracked peppercorns. With very sharp knife, cut each package across centre without cutting through and place on warmed plates. Drizzle with Fresh Ginger Juice Sauce and garnish with salmon roe. *Serves 4.*

*If sorrel is unavailable, substitute spinach leaves.

1/3	cup grated gingerroot
1 1/2	cups boiling water
	pinch cayenne pepper
2	tsp liquid honey
1	tsp unsalted butter

Fresh Ginger Juice Sauce

Place gingerroot in bowl; stir in boiling water and let cool. Strain liquid into small saucepan. Add cayenne pepper and honey; boil until reduced by half. Remove from heat and stir in butter. *Makes 3/4 cup.*

Chef's wine suggestion: British Columbia VQA Chardonnay

GOOD NIGHT SALMON

TOJO'S RESTAURANT, VANCOUVER, BC / *Restaurateur: Hidekazu Tojo*

This special salmon creation with the romantic name is easy to prepare. You may substitute other fresh fish of your choice.

3	tbsp miso paste*
2	tbsp mirin (Japanese rice wine)
2	tbsp sake (Japanese wine)
1	tbsp granulated sugar
1	tsp ground ginger
	dash cayenne pepper
1 1/2	lb sockeye or spring salmon piece, cut in 6-oz portions
2	green onions, chopped
4	shiitake mushrooms, chopped

In bowl, whisk together miso paste, mirin, sake, sugar, ginger and cayenne pepper until smooth. Place fish in shallow dish; pour marinade over top, coating well on all sides. Cover with plastic wrap and marinate in refrigerator for 8 hours.

Remove salmon from marinade, and transfer to baking dish; cook in 350°F oven for 12 to 15 minutes or until fish is opaque.

TO SERVE: Place on warmed plates and garnish with chopped green onions and shiitake mushrooms. Accompany with vegetables of choice Serves 4.

*Fermented soybean paste is available in Asian markets.

Restaurateur's wine suggestion: Tojo's premium sake, Masu Kagam

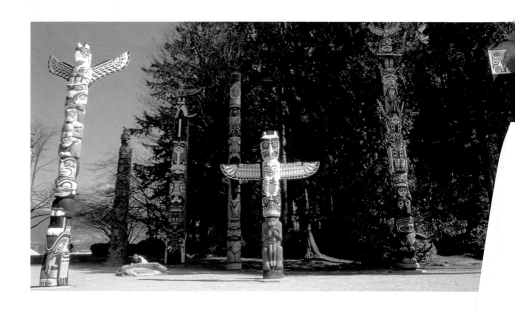

BRIOCHE AND 7 C'S SPICE–CRUSTED PACIFIC LINGCOD

C RESTAURANT, VANCOUVER, BC / *Executive Chef: Robert Clark*

C Restaurant specializes in innovative seafood entrées presented in a dramatic fashion. In this recipe, chef Robert Clark transforms cod into an exotically spiced delicacy served on a bed of julienned red pepper and jícama salad. The 7 C's blend of spices works equally well with pork, chicken and other species of seafood.

1/3	cup brioche crumbs* (or soft bread crumbs, preferably sweet)
2	tsp 7 C's Spice Blend (recipe follows)
1/4	tsp salt
1/4	tsp pepper
2	jícama, peeled and julienned
2	sweet red peppers, seeded and julienned
3	tbsp mayonnaise
1	tsp Dijon mustard
1	tbsp butter
1 1/2	lb lingcod fillets (6-oz portions)
2	lemons, halved
	Tomatillo Emulsion (recipe follows)
1	green onion, sliced
2	tbsp diced pickled beets

In bowl, mix together brioche crumbs, 7 C's Spice Blend, salt and pepper; set aside. In separate bowl, combine jícama, red peppers, mayonnaise and mustard; set aside in refrigerator.

In ovenproof skillet, heat butter over medium-high heat; sear cod on 1 side until golden. Turn over and sprinkle with crumb mixture; cook for 3 minutes. Transfer skillet to 375°F oven and bake for 8 to 10 minutes or until crumb mixture is browned and fish is opaque and flakes easily. Remove from oven; squeeze juice of 1/2 lemon over each fillet.

TO SERVE: Arrange salad in centre of plates; top with fish. Drizzle Tomatillo Emulsion around salad and garnish with green onion and diced pickled beets. *Serves 4.*

Brioche is a sweet French bread made with large amounts of butter and eggs; it is sold in French and specialty bakeries.

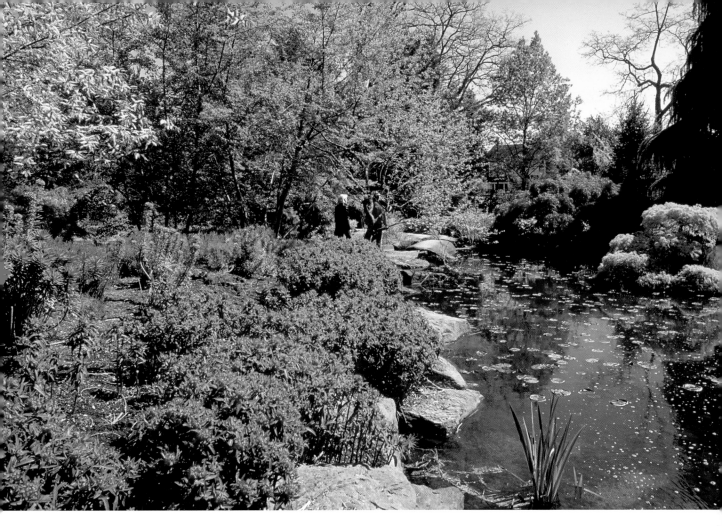

Tomatillo Emulsion

1/2 cup tomatillos*, hull removed, cleaned and diced
2 tbsp vegetable oil
1 tbsp cilantro leaves
salt and pepper

In blender, purée tomatillos, oil and cilantro until smooth. Season with salt and pepper to taste. Set aside until serving. *Makes 1/2 cup.*

A small fruit popular in Mexican and Southwest cooking, tomatillos, or Mexican green tomatoes, as they are also called, are sold in Latin American and specialty grocery stores and some supermarkets.

7 C's Spice Blend

1 tbsp caraway seeds
1 cardamom seeds or ground cardamom
8 whole cloves
2 tbsp ground cumin
2 tbsp ground coriander
1 tbsp chili pepper flakes or powder (ancho, chipotle, red, etc.)
2 tsp cinnamon

In dry skillet over medium heat, toast caraway and cardamom seeds, stirring often to prevent burning, for about 5 minutes or until fragrant. Let cool.

In blender, process seeds, cloves, cumin, coriander, pepper flakes and cinnamon until a fine powder. Let cool and store in airtight container for up to 6 months. *Makes 1/3 cup.*

LUNCH, TEA, BREAKFAST

HERE ARE DELIGHTFUL RECIPES THAT WILL TAKE YOU ON A CULINARY ODYSSEY THROUGHOUT THE DAY, FROM EARLY morning through to afternoon tea.

Chateau Whistler Granola from the slope-side Wildflower Restaurant on Whistler Mountain is filled with nuts, fruits and grains to keep you at a high energy level for hours. For a more leisurely and elegant breakfast/brunch experience, try Orange Cardamom French Toast from Oritalia or Summerhill Smoked Salmon Eggs Benedict from Summerhill Estate Winery.

I have included a trio of creamy rice risottos, each featuring different vegetables: sun-dried tomatoes; chanterelle mushrooms and sweet corn; and pumpkin with saffron. Serve the risottos with a salad and warm crusty bread for a light luncheon.

When you are in the provincial capital, Victoria, you must treat yourself to the experience of afternoon tea at The Empress hotel. This tradition has been carried on at the hotel for generations, and you are invited to recapture the ritual in your own home with an assortment of teatime recipes.

◀ Empress Scones

EMPRESS SCONES

AFTERNOON TEA AT THE EMPRESS HOTEL, VICTORIA, BC / *Executive Chef: David Hammonds*

It's teatime on the West Coast, featuring The Empress Hotel's world-famous scones. An institution at The Empress since 1908, this afternoon repast is prepared for more than 100,000 guests annually. The scones are served hot from the oven with thick cream and homemade strawberry preserves.

3	cups all-purpose flour
1/2	cup granulated sugar
2	tbsp baking powder
1/3	cup butter, softened
3	eggs
1	cup 35% cream
1/3	cup raisins
1	tbsp water
	pinch salt

In bowl, sift together flour, sugar and baking powder. Add butter and blend with fingertips until incorporated and mixture is mealy. (Be careful not to overprocess.) Lightly beat 2 of the eggs and blend into mixture along with cream just until combined.

On floured surface, lightly press batter to 1-inch thickness. With biscuit cutter, cut out scones and place on ungreased baking sheet. Whisk together remaining egg, water and salt to form egg wash; brush over scones and let stand for 45 minutes, uncovered.

Bake in 325°F oven for 20 to 25 minutes or until scones are golden brown. *Makes 1 1/2 dozen.*

CHATEAU WHISTLER GRANOLA

THE WILDFLOWER RESTAURANT AT CP CHATEAU WHISTLER RESORT / *Executive Chef: Glenn Monk*

If all cereal tasted as good as this, then you would rarely find bacon and eggs on the breakfast menu. Wholesome and nutritious, it's just what you need to prepare for a day on the slopes.

4	cups rolled oats
1 2/3	cups chopped pecans
1 1/2	cups wheat bran
1 1/2	cups slivered almonds
1 1/3	cup sunflower seeds
2/3	cup sesame seeds
1/3	cup + 1 tbsp vegetable oil
2 1/2	cups raisins
1 1/2	cups chopped dates
3/4	cup currants
1/3	cup liquid honey
1	tbsp vanilla extract
1	tbsp orange zest

In large bowl, combine rolled oats, pecans, wheat bran, almonds, sunflower seeds and sesame seeds; pour in 1/3 cup oil and stir to coat. Spread on 2 baking sheets; bake in 325°F oven, stirring every 10 minutes, for 30 minutes or until golden. Transfer to large bowl. Add raisins, dates and currants.

Combine honey, vanilla and orange zest; stir into granola until well combined. Let cool completely before storing in airtight container for up to 1 month. *Makes about 3 1/2 lb or 30 servings.*

ORANGE CARDAMOM FRENCH TOAST

ORITALIA, VANCOUVER, BC / EXECUTIVE CHEF: JULIAN BOND

This variation of your mother's French toast will sweep you off your feet. Its citrus flavour with just a hint of exotic cardamom is simply the best!

8	eggs
3/4	cup 10% cream
3	tbsp orange zest
3/4	cup orange juice
2	tbsp Grand Marnier
1 1/2	tsp ground cardamom
1	loaf white country bread or fruit bread, thickly sliced
2 to 3	tbsp butter
	fresh seasonal berries
	icing sugar
	maple syrup, warmed

In bowl, beat together eggs, cream, liqueur, orange zest, orange juice and Grand Marnier. Stir in cardamom and let stand for 1 hour.

Soak bread slices in egg mixture. In skillet, heat 1 tbsp butter over medium heat; fry bread slices for 2 to 3 minutes per side or until golden and centre is cooked. Repeat for remaining slices adding more butter to skillet as necessary.

TO SERVE: Top French Toast with berries, dusting of icing sugar and warmed maple syrup. *Serves 4 to 6.*

SUMMERHILL SMOKED SALMON EGGS BENEDICT

SMOKEHAUS VERANDA RESTAURANT AT SUMMERHILL ESTATE WINERY, KELOWNA, BC / *Chef: Graham Pierce*

Eggs Benedict is traditionally served with ham and Hollandaise Sauce. But you will never settle for the traditional once you savour Smoked Salmon Eggs Benedict from the kitchen at Summerhill Estate Winery. It is warm and succulent, with a delicious Hollandaise and generous chunks of hot-smoked salmon prepared on site. Serve with a side salad and garnish of choice.

2	English muffins, sliced
	butter
4	oz smoked salmon
	water
1	tsp vinegar
4	eggs
	Hollandaise Sauce (recipe follows)

Lightly toast muffins; spread with butter. Top with smoked salmon and keep warm in oven.

In saucepan large enough to poach all eggs, combine water and vinegar; bring to simmer. Crack eggs and gently slip into water; poach to desired doneness. Remove with slotted spoon, draining excess water. Place on muffins and top with Hollandaise Sauce. *Serves 4.*

Hollandaise Sauce

2	egg yolks
2	tsp white wine
	pinch salt
	dash Tabasco Sauce
1/2	cup clarified unsalted butter, melted

In top of double boiler over simmering water, beat together egg yolks, wine, salt and Tabasco; cook, whisking constantly, for 6 to 8 minutes or until mixture begins to thicken enough to coat back of spoon. Slowly whisk in melted butter. Remove from heat and keep warm. *Makes 3/4 cup.*

Chef's wine suggestion: Summerhill Chardonnay 1998

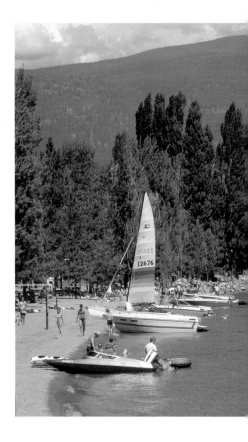

SPRING MUSHROOM CANNELLONI

THE AERIE RESORT, MALAHAT, BC / *Chef de Cuisine: Chris Jones*

This lunch or light dinner entrée tastes wonderful and, as an added bonus, it makes an interesting presentation for guests. The cannelloni are cut on the bias and positioned to stand up in a splash of herbed stock and rich yellow extra-virgin olive oil.

3	sheets fresh herb pasta, 10 x 4 inches*
3	tbsp vegetable oil
	salt
1	onion, chopped
2	cloves garlic, minced
3	cups chopped mushrooms (combination morel, oyster and/or cremini)
1/2	cup dry white wine
1/2	cup rich chicken stock**
1 1/2	cups coarse bread crumbs
1 1/2	tbsp chopped fresh rosemary
2 or 3	eggs, beaten
	pepper
	Herbed Chicken Stock (recipe follows)
	extra-virgin olive oil
1	cup shaved sheep's milk cheese or Parmigiano-Reggiano cheese

Cut pasta sheets crosswise in 3 equal parts. Fill large pot three-quarters full of water; add 1/2 tsp of the vegetable oil and pinch of salt. Bring to boil. Blanch pasta in boiling water until slightly underdone, 4 to 8 minutes depending on type of pasta. Drain and let cool in ice water. Lightly oil pasta; place on baking sheet, cover with plastic wrap and set aside.

In skillet, heat remaining vegetable oil over medium heat; cook onion and garlic, stirring often, for about 4 to 5 minutes or until softened. Add mushrooms and sauté, stirring constantly, for about 5 minutes or until tender and light golden. Deglaze skillet with wine and chicken stock; continue to cook for about 10 to 12 minutes or until liquid is completely evaporated. Transfer to bowl and let cool. Stir in bread crumbs, rosemary and enough egg to moisten. Season with salt and pepper to taste.

Spoon mushroom mixture along 1 short end of each pasta sheet; roll up to diameter of 1 inch. Wrap each cannelloni tightly in plastic wrap and tie ends with twine to seal cannelloni for final cooking. You will have 9 individual rolls.

Bring large pot of water to boil; add wrapped cannelloni. Reduce heat to simmer and poach for 7 to 10 minutes or until firm. Drain; carefully unwrap cannelloni and keep warm.

TO SERVE: Cut each cannelloni in half on diagonal. Place 6 cannelloni halves, flat end down, upright in centre of each of 6 warmed plates. Lay remaining cannelloni on plates for a total of 3 per serving. Surround with Herbed Chicken Stock and extra-virgin olive oil; top with shaved cheese. *Serves 6.*

Fresh pasta sheets are available in most food stores.

** *To make rich chicken stock, heat canned sodium-reduced chicken broth over medium heat and reduce by half.*

1 1/2	cups sodium-reduced chicken broth
	handful fresh herbs (any combination of rosemary, oregano, basil, thyme)

Herbed Chicken Stock

In small saucepan, bring chicken broth and herbs to boil; reduce heat to medium-low and simmer until reduced by half. Set aside. Makes 3/4 cup.

FRITTATA TRATTORIA

TRATTORIA DI UMBERTO RESTAURANT, WHISTLER, BC / *Owner: Umberto Menghi*

This traditional Italian omelette sports a goat cheese, mushroom and roasted sweet pepper flavour with just a hint of basil. Serve it for breakfast or add a small salad for a luncheon dish.

1	sweet red pepper
6	eggs
1	tbsp chopped fresh basil (or 1/2 tsp dried)
	pinch salt
	pepper
1	tsp olive oil
1/2	cup button or cremini mushrooms, sliced
1/2	cup goat cheese (chèvre), crumbled

On grill over high heat, roast red pepper, turning often, for 8 to 10 minutes or until skin is charred. Remove from heat and let cool in paper bag. Remove skin; core, and seed. Chop pepper and set aside.

In large bowl, beat together eggs, basil, salt and pepper; set aside. In ovenproof skillet, heat oil over medium heat; sauté mushroom and red pepper for 4 minutes. Stir into egg mixture along with goat cheese.

In same skillet, cook egg mixture over medium heat for 3 minutes. Transfer skillet to 375°F oven and cook for 8 to 10 minutes or until desired firmness is reached. *Serves 4.*

Chef's wine suggestion: Sumac Ridge Pinot Blanc VQA, 1998

SUN-DRIED TOMATO RISOTTO

VAL D'ISÈRE RESTAURANT, WHISTLER, BC / *Owner/Chef: Roland Pfaff*

At Val d'Isère, chef Roland Pfaff serves this risotto as an accompaniment to his cedar-infused salmon entrée. It works equally well as a light vegetarian main course served with a crisp salad and crusty French bread.

4	tbsp unsalted butter
4	tbsp minced shallots
2	tbsp minced garlic
1	cup Arborio rice*
2 1/2 to 3 cups vegetable stock	
3	tbsp tomato paste
3	tbsp chopped dry-packed sun-dried tomatoes
3	tbsp diced tomatoes
3	tbsp grated Parmesan cheese (approx)
	salt and pepper
	sprigs fresh herbs

In saucepan, melt butter over low heat; cook shallots and garlic, covered, for 5 minutes. Add rice and cook, stirring constantly, until grains are slightly transparent. Pour in 1/2 cup vegetable stock; cook, stirring often and adding remaining stock 1/2 cup at a time, allowing rice to completely absorb liquid each time, for about 25 minutes or until rice is almost tender. Add tomato paste and cook for 4 to 5 minutes or until creamy and al dente. Stir in sun-dried tomatoes, diced tomatoes and Parmesan cheese; season with salt and pepper to taste.

TO SERVE: Mound slightly on plates or in shallow bowls; garnish with fresh herbs and additional Parmesan cheese. *Serves 4.*

*Italian-grown Arborio rice is thicker and shorter than other short-grain rice and has a higher starch content.

SAFFRON RISOTTO WITH PUMPKIN

IL GIARDINO AND UMBERTO'S, VANCOUVER, BC / *Owner: Umberto Menghi*

"Home cooking away from home" is the motto of most Italian restaurants, and Umberto Menghi's Il Giardino is no exception. Rich aromas waft through the restaurant and out into the street, beckoning hungry passersby. A traditional creamy rice risotto is always on the menu at Il Giardino, and this version, with its subtle saffron flavour and diced colourful pumpkin, makes a fine luncheon dish.

1	marrow bone, 3 to 4 inches long, refrigerated
3	tbsp olive oil
2	shallots, minced
1 3/4	cups fresh pie pumpkin, peeled, seeded and finely diced (do not use canned)
1 1/3	cups Arborio rice*
1/4	cup white wine
4	cups chicken stock
1/4	cup grated Parmesan cheese (approx)
1	tbsp butter
1	tsp chopped fresh parsley
	large pinch saffron
	salt and white pepper
	sprigs fresh parsley

With spoon, remove marrow from bone and dice. In saucepan, heat oil over low heat; cook shallots, covered for 5 minutes. Increase heat to medium; add diced marrow and pumpkin and cook for 2 minutes. Add rice; cook, stirring constantly, until grains are slightly transparent. Pour in wine and stir until absorbed. Pour in enough stock to come 1/2 inch above rice. Simmer, stirring frequently and adding stock as necessary to keep rice covered, 25 to 30 minutes or until rice is almost tender. Add Parmesan cheese, butter, chopped parsley and saffron; cook for 4 to 5 minutes or until creamy but al dente. Season with salt and pepper to taste.

TO SERVE: Mound slightly on serving plates or in large pasta bowls. Garnish with additional Parmesan cheese and parsley sprigs. *Serves 4.*

*Italian-grown Arborio rice is thicker and shorter than other short-grain rice and has a higher starch content.

Chef's wine suggestion: Hawthorne Mountain Vineyards Gewürztraminer VQA, 1997

PORTOBELLO MUSHROOM CUTLETS WITH BALSAMIC SAUCE AND ROASTED BABY VEGETABLES

BIN 941 TAPAS PARLOUR, VANCOUVER, BC / *Owner/Chef: Gord Martin*

Chef Gord Martin is skilled at blending diverse flavours, colours and textures in his dishes, turning the ordinary into a memorable repast. This portobello mushroom tapatiser is one of the signature selections at BIN 941.

4	large portobello mushrooms, stems removed
4	tbsp olive oil
2	tbsp balsamic vinegar
	salt and pepper
1	egg
1	cup milk
1/2	cup all-purpose flour
3	cups panko* (or dry bread crumbs)
	Balsamic Sauce (recipe follows)
1	tbsp butter
1	head roasted garlic**
	Roasted Baby Vegetables (recipe follows)

Spread mushrooms on baking sheet: sprinkle with half of the oil, the balsamic vinegar and salt and pepper to taste. Bake in 400°F oven for 10 minutes; turn and bake for 10 minutes longer. Remove from oven and let cool.

Lightly beat egg and milk to make egg wash. Dredge mushrooms in flour, dip in egg wash and coat with panko, pressing to adhere. In large ovenproof skillet, heat remaining oil and add mushrooms; transfer to 425°F oven and bake for 10 minutes. Turn mushrooms and bake for 10 minutes longer or until coating is crisp. Transfer to plate and keep warm.

Heat same skillet over medium heat; cook Balsamic Sauce, butter and roasted garlic, whisking until butter is dissolved.

TO SERVE: Centre mushrooms on each of 4 warmed plates; top with Roasted Baby Vegetables and drizzle with Balsamic Sauce mixture. *Serves 4.*

Panko crumbs are coarse Japanese bread crumbs and are available in Asian markets.

**To roast garlic: Separate and peel cloves of 1 head garlic. Bake on baking sheet in 350°F oven for 20 to 25 minutes until soft and brown.*

1 1/4	cups balsamic vinegar
1	tbsp granulated sugar
1	tsp cornstarch
1 1/2	tbsp water

Balsamic Sauce

In small saucepan over medium heat, cook balsamic vinegar until reduced by half. Combine sugar, cornstarch and water; whisk into vinegar and cook, stirring constantly, for 3 to 5 minutes or until slightly thickened. Set aside. *Makes 2/3 cup.*

Roasted Baby Vegetables

2	tbsp olive oil
2	cups baby vegetables (combination of baby carrots, zucchini and squash), sliced lengthwise
1	cup French beans, sliced lengthwise
2	baby bok choy, sliced
1/2	sweet red pepper, julienned
1	tbsp zatar*

In ovenproof skillet, heat olive oil over medium-high heat; cook baby vegetables, beans, bok choy, red pepper and zatar, stirring to coat, for 2 to 3 minutes. Transfer to 425°F oven and bake, turning occasionally, for 15 minutes or until browned. Set aside and keep warm.

Zatar is a Greek and Middle Eastern seasoning of thyme, salt and sesame seeds found in Mediterranean specialty shops.

CHANTERELLE AND SWEET CORN RISOTTO

BISHOP'S RESTAURANT, VANCOUVER, BC / *Owner/Executive Chef: Dennis Green*

This creamy risotto works well as an accompaniment to a favourite entrée or as a main-course vegetarian dish. The beautiful trumpet-shaped chanterelle mushroom is found in the wild in the Pacific Northwest. If fresh chanterelles are not available, you may substitute any of the more exotic wild mushrooms, such as enoki, morel or shiitake, but you will not achieve the delicate light orange colour.

3	tbsp butter
1	cup diced onions
1	large clove garlic, minced
1/4	cup chopped fresh sage
2	cups chanterelle mushrooms
2	cups Arborio rice*
1/2	cup dry white wine
1	cup corn kernels
4	cups chicken stock
1	cup 35% cream
1	cup small fresh spinach leaves
1/4	cup grated Parmesan cheese (approx)
	salt and pepper
	sprigs fresh sage

In saucepan, melt butter over low heat; cook onions, garlic and sage, covered for 5 minutes. Add mushrooms and sauté for 1 to 2 minutes or until lightly coloured. Add rice and sauté for 2 to 3 minutes or until grains are slightly transparent. Deglaze pan with wine. Add corn and enough stock to cover rice by 1/2 inch. Simmer, stirring often and adding more stock as necessary to keep rice covered, for about 30 minutes or until rice is almost tender. Add cream, spinach and Parmesan cheese and cook for 4 to 5 minutes or until creamy but al dente. Season with salt and pepper to taste.

TO SERVE: Mound slightly on serving plates and garnish with sage sprigs and additional Parmesan cheese. *Serves 6.*

Italian-grown Arborio rice is thicker and shorter than other short-grain rice and has a higher starch content.

MOUNT CURRIE RHUBARB AND SWEET GINGER CHUTNEY

THE WILDFLOWER RESTAURANT AT CP CHATEAU WHISTLER RESORT / *Executive Chef: Glenn Monk*

It is the policy at Chateau Whistler Resort to utilize locally grown produce whenever possible. This delicious gingery condiment features ripe red rhubarb grown in nearby Pemberton, at the base of snow-capped Mount Currie. It works well as an accompaniment to cheese and crackers, savoury biscuits and with pork, chicken or fish dishes.

4	tbsp vegetable oil
2	cups chopped onion
1 1/2	tsp diced gingerroot
2	tsp minced garlic
2	tsp curry paste*
4	lb rhubarb, peeled and cut into 1-inch cubes
1	cup raisins
1 1/2	cups packed brown sugar
1 1/2	cups cider vinegar
1	tsp salt

In large pot, heat oil over medium heat; sweat onions for 4 to 5 minutes. Add ginger, garlic and curry paste; cook, stirring often, for 4 to 5 minutes or until onions are softened. Stir in rhubarb and raisins; add sugar and stir until dissolved.

Add vinegar and salt; reduce heat to low and simmer for 30 minutes. Remove from heat; pour into hot sterilized jars and seal. *Makes about 6 cups.*

*Curry paste is available in the specialty section of most supermarkets and in Asian food stores.

CUCUMBER SANDWICHES

AFTERNOON TEA AT THE EMPRESS HOTEL, VICTORIA, BC / *Executive Chef: David Hammonds*

What would a Victorian afternoon tea be without the traditional thinly sliced cucumber sandwich? Simple to prepare, yes, but a definite must for proper tea etiquette.

8	thin slices white bread
2	tbsp butter, softened
2	tbsp mayonnaise
1	English cucumber, peeled and thinly sliced
	salt and pepper

Spread all bread slices with butter and mayonnaise. Arrange sliced cucumber on 4 of the bread slices; season with salt and pepper to taste. Top with remaining bread slices. Trim crusts and cut into 4 squares, rectangles or triangles. *Serves 4.*

ALMOND CRACKERS

QUATTRO AT WHISTLER, WHISTLER, BC / *Executive Chef: Rob Parrott*

Chef Rob Parrott serves these delightful little bites with anise pistachio ice cream as an accompaniment to his Chocolate Terrine dessert. They are tasty, appealing to the eye and a versatile addition to a wide variety of desserts as well as to an afternoon tea tray.

2	cups all-purpose flour
1/2	tsp baking soda
	pinch salt
1/3	cup granulated sugar
1/3	cup liquid honey
1/4	cup butter, softened
2	tsp vegetable oil
1	egg white
1 1/2	tsp vanilla extract
1	tsp almond extract
1/4	cup sliced almonds

In bowl, sift together flour, baking soda and salt. Set aside.

Using mixer on medium speed, cream sugar, honey, butter and oil until well blended. Add egg white, vanilla and almond extract; beat just until blended. Stir in flour mixture until combined (dough will be sticky).

Divide dough into 2 equal portions. Shape each into 9-inch log; wrap in plastic wrap and freeze until firm.

Cut each log into 1/4-inch slices and place 1 inch apart on greased baking sheet. Top each with sliced almond, pressing lightly to adhere. Bake in 350°F oven for 6 to 8 minutes or until lightly browned. Transfer to racks and let cool. *Makes 6 dozen.*

DESSERTS

I BELIEVE THAT IT IS IMPOSSIBLE TO CREATE A TRULY DECADENT DESSERT WITHOUT CREAM, BUTTER AND SUGAR. THOSE WHO claim it can be done never seem to be able to completely satisfy the sweet-tooth cravings of true die-hard dessert lovers. My motto is "Indulge with moderation." Serve smaller dessert portions and limit their frequency. Enjoy fresh fruit most days of the week and live it up occasionally with one of these delicious dessert recipes.

Chocolate lovers will rave over the silky smooth Chocolate Terrine from Quattro at Whistler and will testify that Boca Negra from The Mahle House Restaurant has to be the best chocolate cake ever created.

When rhubarb first appears in your garden and at local markets, you know spring is here and summer is not far off. To herald the season, make the sweet little Rhubarb Upside-Down Cakes from Bishop's Restaurant or the Stilton Cheesecake with Rhubarb Compote from Diva at the Met Restaurant. Contributing chefs take full advantage of the wonderful summer fruits and berries available to them in British Columbia and have offered us a variety of delectable ways to enjoy them. Treat family and friends to Fresh Berries with Ginger-Scented Mascarpone, or Stone Fruit Clafouti with Toasted Hazelnuts, which features a trio of fresh Okanagan Valley fruits, from The Amphora Restaurant at Hainle Vineyards Estate Winery.

Many of these recipes include additional sauces, creams and garnishes and I encourage you to be as resourceful as our contributing chefs: mix and match different components and ingredients according to what is in season or what you have on hand. I am sure you will enjoy creating these delicious recipes and that you will make them over and over again.

◀ Sunburnt Lemon Pie

SUNBURNT LEMON PIE

SEASONS RESTAURANT IN QUEEN ELIZABETH PARK, VANCOUVER, BC / *Executive Chef: Pierre Delacote*

Serve this classic dessert garnished with a variety of fresh fruit slices and berries. The fruit will provide a lovely contrast in colour and taste.

1 1/2 cups	all-purpose flour
1/3 cup + 1 tbsp	granulated sugar
1/2 cup	butter, softened
1	egg
1 tsp	orange zest
1 tbsp	orange juice
	Lemon Filling (recipe follows)

Pastry

In bowl, combine flour and 1/3 cup sugar. Mix in butter with fingertips until crumbly, being careful not to overprocess. In small bowl, whisk together egg, orange zest and juice. With fork, stir egg mixture into flour mixture just until ball forms. Wrap in plastic wrap and refrigerate for 20 minutes.

On lightly floured surface, roll out pastry to uniform thickness of 1/4 inch. Press into lightly greased 10-inch pie plate. Cover with parchment paper and fill with pie weights. Bake in 350°F oven for 20 minutes or until centre is set. Lift out parchment with weights. Cool.

Pour Lemon Filling into pastry shell; bake for 30 minutes. Remove from oven and let cool. Cover edges of crust with foil, sprinkle remaining 1 tbsp sugar evenly over tart surface and broil for 3 to 4 minutes or until sugar is caramelized. (Watch carefully to make sure pie does not burn.) *Serves 8 to 12.*

Lemon filling
(prepare while shell is cooling)

6	eggs
3/4 cup	granulated sugar
3/4 cup	35% cream
1 tsp	lemon zest
1/2 cup	lemon juice
1 1/2 tsp	vanilla extract

With mixer, beat eggs and sugar until pale. Add cream, lemon zest and juice and vanilla; beat until smooth. Set aside until pie shell is cooled.

STONE FRUIT CLAFOUTI WITH TOASTED HAZELNUTS

THE AMPHORA BISTRO AT HAINLE VINEYARDS ESTATE WINERY, PEACHLAND, BC / *Executive Chef: David Forestell*

Clafouti, traditionally made with cherries, is varied at The Amphora Bistro to showcase locally grown Okanagan Gold Bar apricots, Red Haven peaches and the highly prized but rare Southern Belle White nectarines.

4	apricots, 2 peaches and 2 nectarines
4	eggs
6	tbsp granulated sugar
3/4	cup milk
2	tbsp Frangelico
2	tsp vanilla
1/2	cup all-purpose flour
	pinch salt
2	tbsp unsalted butter
1/3	cup toasted hazelnuts*, coarsely chopped
1	cup 35% cream, whipped
	icing sugar

Plunge fruit into pot of boiling water for 30 seconds so that skins can be easily removed. Cut apricots into quarters, peaches into eighths and nectarines into sixths. Set aside.

In large bowl, whisk eggs and 4 tbsp of the sugar until volume is almost tripled. Add milk, Frangelico, and vanilla; whisk to combine. Sift flour and salt over top; whisk vigorously until no lumps remain.

Place butter in well-seasoned 10-inch cast-iron skillet; heat in 450°F oven until butter just begins to brown. Remove skillet from oven; quickly pour in batter. Cover with fruit pieces and sprinkle with hazelnuts and remaining sugar.

Return skillet to oven, reduce heat to 400°F and bake for 25 to 30 minutes or until deep golden brown and toothpick inserted in centre comes out clean. Let cool until just warm and serve with dollop of whipped cream and dusting of icing sugar. *Serves 6 to 8.*

*To toast hazelnuts: Spread nuts in single layer on baking sheet; bake in 350oF oven for 10 to 15 minutes or until golden. Immediately wrap in clean tea towel and rub to remove skins. Let cool; chop coarsely.

Chef's wine suggestion: British Columbia late-harvest Riesling or icewine

FRESH BERRIES WITH GINGER-SCENTED MASCARPONE, CITRUS CURD AND PISTACHIO TUILE TOWERS

THE AERIE RESORT, MALAHAT, BC / *Executive Chef: Chris Jones*

This exceptional dessert offers the home chef a variety of options. Each sub-recipe is interchangeable and may be combined with other dessert recipes. For example, the ginger-scented mascarpone can be served alone, accompanied by the citrus curd or a berry coulis. The pistachio towers can be filled with whipped cream, ice cream or a flavoured mousse. The chef notes that some of the recipes will make more than 4 to 6 portions, but this is necessary to successfully complete the recipes. Extra tuiles can be frozen for later use.

	Pistachio Tuiles (recipe follows)
	Ginger-Scented Mascarpone Mousse (recipe follows)
2	cups fresh seasonal berries of choice (raspberries, blueberries, strawberries, blackberries)
	Citrus Curd (recipe follows)
	icing sugar
	mint leaves

Fill tuiles half full with Ginger-Scented Mascarpone Mousse; top with some of the berries. Mound small amount of remaining mousse onto centre of each of 6 dessert plates and stand tuile(s) upright in centre. Garnish with Citrus Curd and additional berries. Dust with icing sugar and garnish with mint. *Serves 6.*

Ginger-Scented Mascarpone Mousse

2	tbsp liquid honey
1	tsp finely minced gingerroot
8	oz mascarpone cheese, at room temperature
1/2	cup 35% cream

In small saucepan, heat honey and ginger over medium heat; cook, stirring, until reduced slightly. Remove from heat and let cool.

Fold honey mixture into mascarpone cheese until well blended. In mixer, whip cream until stiff peaks form; gently fold in mascarpone cheese mixture. Cover and refrigerate until using. *Makes 1 1/2 cups.*

Citrus Curd

	zest and juice of 2 lemons
	zest and juice of 2 oranges
	zest and juice of 1 lime
3/4	cup granulated sugar
6	egg yolks

In top of double boiler over simmering water, whisk together lemon, orange and lime zest and juice, sugar and egg yolks; cook, whisking vigorously, for 8 to 10 minutes or until thickened. Strain through fine-mesh strainer and refrigerate to chill. *Makes 1 1/2 cups.*

Pistachio Tuiles

3/4 cup unsalted butter, softened
1/2 cup granulated sugar
3 egg whites
3/4 cup all-purpose flour
1/4 cup ground pistachio nuts

With mixer, cream butter and sugar until light and fluffy. With mixer running, add egg whites, 1 at a time; gradually add flour until blended. Let stand for 2 to 3 hours.

Line baking sheet with parchment paper. Spread batter on paper in thin 4 x 2-inch rectangles. Sprinkle with pistachio nuts and bake in 350°F oven for 5 to 6 minutes until light golden. Remove from oven; with spatula, quickly lift tuiles from pan and drape each around 3/4-inch diameter dowel, pressing edges to adhere, to create 2-inch high cylinders. Let cool and set aside. *Makes 2 dozen.*

WARM RAIN FOREST CRUNCH BANANA WITH HOT CHOCOLATE SAUCE

HERALD STREET CAFFE, VICTORIA, BC / *Executive Chef: Mark Finnigan*

The combination of crunchy phyllo bananas drizzled in a warm chocolate sauce and nestled against cold ice cream sends taste buds into ecstasy.

1/2	cup toasted pecans*, chopped
1/2	cup toasted coconut*
2	large ripe bananas, peeled and cut in half crosswise
4	sheets phyllo pastry
1/2	cup butter, melted
	vanilla bean ice cream
	Hot Chocolate Sauce (recipe follows)
	icing sugar

In bowl, combine nuts and coconut. Roll banana halves in nut mixture, pressing firmly to coat well. Set aside.

Place 1 sheet of phyllo on work surface and brush with butter. Top with second sheet, brush with butter and cut phyllo stack in half crosswise. Lay 2 of the bananas on ends of phyllo rectangles; roll up, folding in sides. Repeat with remaining phyllo, butter and bananas.

Brush banana rolls with melted butter and bake in 350°F oven for 10 minutes or until pastry is golden brown.

TO SERVE: Cut rolls in half on angle. On each of 4 dessert plates place 1 half upright and another on its side. Scoop vanilla bean ice cream next to rolls. Drizzle with Hot Chocolate Sauce and dust with icing sugar. *Serves 4.*

To toast pecans and coconut: Spread nuts and coconut on separate baking sheets and bake in 350°F oven, stirring or shaking pans often, for 10 to 12 minutes or until golden and fragrant. Let cool.

Hot Chocolate Sauce

5	oz bittersweet chocolate, finely chopped
1	cup 35% cream
2	tbsp unsalted butter

Place chocolate in bowl. Bring cream to boil and pour over chocolate. Add butter and whisk until chocolate is melted. *Makes 1 cup.*

Chef's wine suggestion: British Columbia Riesling Icewine

RHUBARB UPSIDE-DOWN CAKES

BISHOP'S RESTAURANT, VANCOUVER, BC / *Executive Chef: Dennis Green*

Rhubarb has traditionally heralded the beginning of spring and the arrival of fresh produce after a lingering winter season. Though treated as a fruit, this tart vegetable is actually a member of the buckwheat family. In this dessert from Bishop's Restaurant, the rhubarb becomes slightly caramelized with the brown sugar when baked in a buttery orange cake. Serve warm with a dollop of whipped cream or vanilla bean ice cream.

1	lb rhubarb
1/4	cup butter, melted
2/3	cup packed brown sugar
1/2	cup butter, softened
1/2	cup granulated sugar
2	eggs
1 1/2	cups all-purpose flour
1	tsp baking powder
1/2	tsp baking soda
1/2	tsp salt
	zest and juice of 1 orange
1/2	cup milk

Cut rhubarb stalks in half horizontally and slice into 1/2-inch pieces. Brush each of 6 large (10 oz) ramekins with melted butter; sprinkle with brown sugar. Cover bottom of ramekins with sliced rhubarb.

In bowl, cream butter and granulated sugar until light and fluffy. Beat in eggs, mixing well. Sift together flour, baking powder, baking soda and salt; mix into butter mixture alternately with orange zest, juice and milk. Fill ramekins two-thirds full with batter; bake in 350°F oven for 25 to 30 minutes or until tops are golden. Let cool for 10 minutes.

TO SERVE: Run sharp knife around edge of each cake to loosen and invert onto individual dessert plates. *Serves 6.*

STILTON CHEESECAKE WITH RHUBARB COMPOTE

DIVA AT THE MET, VANCOUVER, BC / *Executive Chef: Michael Noble*

This is quite possibly one of the best cheesecakes ever! Executive chef Michael Noble marries in perfect harmony his distinctive creamy blue cheese filling with a melt-in-your-mouth buttery crust. This dessert received GQ Magazine's Top Taste Award for 1997 from food writer Alan Richman. Feel free to substitute other seasonal fruit for the rhubarb.

Shortbread Base

1 1/3	cups all-purpose flour
3	tbsp granulated sugar
1/2	cup less 1 tbsp butter, softened

With mixer, blend together flour and sugar. Beat in butter until blended, being careful not to overprocess. Lightly press dough over bottom of greased 8-inch springform pan. Bake in 350°F oven for 8 to 10 minutes or until golden brown. Remove from oven and let cool.

Filling

24	oz cream cheese, softened
4	oz Stilton cheese, softened
1	cup + 1 tbsp granulated sugar
2	tsp vanilla extract
1/3	cup all-purpose flour
4	eggs
1	cup sour cream
	Rhubarb Compote (recipe follows)

With mixer, blend cream cheese, Stilton cheese, 1 cup sugar and vanilla until smooth. Mix in flour, then eggs, 1 at a time, beating well after each addition. Add sour cream and mix until smooth. Pour into cooled crust and bake in 300°F oven for about 1 hour or until centre is just firm to the touch. Remove from oven, run knife around edge of pan and let cool at room temperature. Cover and refrigerate until serving.

To serve, sprinkle cheesecake with remaining 1 tbsp sugar and broil for about 3 to 4 minutes or until lightly browned. (Watch carefully to ensure that top does not burn.) Let sugar topping cool; slice into wedges. Serve with spoonful of Rhubarb Compote. Serves 12 to 14.

Rhubarb Compote

1/2	cup granulated sugar (approx)
1/4	cup port
12	dry pink peppercorns, crushed
3	cups diced rhubarb

In saucepan, combine sugar, port and peppercorns; bring to boil and cook until reduced by half. Add rhubarb, reduce heat to low and simmer until rhubarb is softened slightly. Taste and adjust sweetness if necessary by adding more sugar. Refrigerate until serving. *Makes 2 cups.*

Chef's wine suggestion: Gold Campbell Port, 1983

CHOCOLATE TERRINE

QUATTRO AT WHISTLER, WHISTLER, BC / *Executive Chef: Rob Parrott*

This smooth-as-silk dessert is a chocolate lover's dream. The chefs at Quattro at Whistler serve it with almond cookies and pistachio anise ice cream but you can garnish it with crème anglaise, sweetened whipped cream or a fruit sauce.

6	oz semisweet chocolate, chopped
3/4	cup butter, cubed
1 1/2	tbsp very strong espresso coffee
6	egg yolks
3/4	cup superfine sugar*
1	cup cocoa powder, sifted
1 1/2	tbsp Cointreau
2	cups 35% cream

In top of double boiler over simmering water, stir together chocolate, butter and espresso until melted and smooth. Remove from heat.

With mixer, whisk egg yolks and sugar until mixture falls in ribbons. Fold in chocolate mixture until well blended. Fold in cocoa and Cointreau.

Whip cream until stiff peaks form. Gently fold into chocolate mixture. Pour into 8- x 4-inch loaf pan lined with plastic wrap. Cover with plastic wrap and refrigerate for 12 hours.

TO SERVE: Unmould terrine on flat surface; gently remove plastic wrap. Slice into serving-size portions. *Serves 8 to 10.*

Make your own superfine sugar by processing regular granulated white sugar in a food processor for a few minutes or until crystals are smaller.

WHITE CHOCOLATE CRÈME BRULÉE

THE MAHLE HOUSE RESTAURANT, NANAIMO, BC / *Owner/Chef: Maureen Loucks*

Save room for dessert when these crème brulées are on the menu. They are absolutely decadent, so you would be well advised not to count the calories! To serve, place custard cups on dessert plate and garnish with chocolate curls, fresh fruit and/or mint sprigs.

5	egg yolks
1/3	cup + 1 tbsp granulated sugar
2	cups 35% cream
3	oz good-quality white chocolate, finely chopped
1/4	tsp vanilla extract

In bowl, whisk together egg yolks and 1/4 cup of the sugar. In top of double boiler over simmering water, heat cream and remaining sugar, stirring constantly. Add white chocolate, whisking until melted and smooth. Gradually whisk hot chocolate into yolk mixture; stir in vanilla.

Ladle cream equally into 6 6-oz custard cups. Place cups in large baking pan and carefully add enough hot water to come halfway up sides of cups. Bake in 325°F oven 45 to 50 minutes until set and golden on top. *Serves 6.*

CARAMELIZED APPLE AND PHYLLO TOWER WITH CRÈME ANGLAISE AND EASY CARAMEL SAUCE

THE WESLEY STREET, NANAIMO, BC / *Executive Chef: Ian Ter Veer*

This impressive dessert is a combination of taste sensations: the crunchiness of phyllo, the sweet-tart flavour of warm apples, the silkiness of crème anglaise and caramel sauce, and cold vanilla ice cream.

2/3	cup butter, melted
2/3	cup granulated sugar
4	sheets phyllo pastry
4	Granny Smith apples
	Easy Caramel Sauce (recipe follows)
	Crème Anglaise (recipe follows)
	vanilla ice cream

Set aside 2 tbsp of the butter and 2 tbsp of the sugar. Place 1 sheet of phyllo on work surface with 1 short edge facing you; butter bottom half of phyllo and sprinkle with sugar. Fold unbuttered half over buttered half and repeat buttering and sugaring one more time until phyllo is folded into quarters. Butter and sugar top of phyllo quarter; cut into 4 equal pieces. Repeat with remaining 3 sheets of phyllo to make a total of 16 layered squares. Place on baking sheets and bake in 375°F oven for 3 to 6 minutes or until golden. (Watch carefully; phyllo burns easily.) Remove from oven and set aside.

Slice top and bottom from apples and slice each into 4 rings of equal thickness. Remove core from centres, being careful not to break rings. In skillet over medium heat, combine reserved butter and sugar. Add apples and sauté until caramelized, turning often for even cooking.

TO SERVE: Place 1 layered phyllo square on each of 4 large dessert plates; top with apple ring. Repeat until there are 4 phyllo-apple layers on each plate. Garnish with Easy Caramel Sauce, Crème Anglaise and vanilla ice cream. *Serves 4.*

2	cups 35% cream
6	egg yolks
2/3	cup granulated sugar
2	tsp vanilla extract

Crème Anglaise

You may create a lighter sauce with less fat content if you substitute milk, 10% cream or a combination for the 35% cream in this recipe.

In top of double boiler over simmering water, heat cream until scalding. In bowl, beat egg yolks and sugar until pale; very gradually add cream, whisking constantly. Return to double boiler; add vanilla and cook, stirring constantly, for about 10 minutes or until thick enough to coat back of spoon. Immediately transfer to bowl and set in pan of ice water to cool, stirring occasionally. *Makes 2 cups.*

Easy Caramel Sauce

1/4 cup butter
1 cup 35% cream
1/2 cup packed brown sugar
2 tbsp light corn syrup
1 tsp vanilla extract

In small saucepan, melt butter over medium heat; add cream, sugar, corn syrup and vanilla and bring to boil, stirring. Boil hard, stirring constantly, for 5 minutes. Let cool for 10 minutes; pour into bowl; cover and refrigerate for up to 1 week. *Makes 1 cup.*

Chef's wine suggestion: British Columbia icewine of choice

BOCA NEGRA

THE MAHLE HOUSE RESTAURANT, NANAIMO, BC / *Owner/Chef: Maureen Loucks*

Chef Maureen Loucks provided one "extra" dessert recipe because she feels that it is incredible and "must be shared." No doubt you will agree it is the best chocolate cake you have ever tasted. A little goes a long way as it is very rich. Prepare the White Chocolate Cream one day in advance to allow flavours to blend.

1 1/3	cups granulated sugar
1/3	cup water
4	tbsp bourbon
12	oz good-quality semisweet chocolate, finely chopped
1	cup unsalted butter, cubed
5	eggs
2	tbsp all-purpose flour
	white and dark chocolate curls for garnish (optional)
	White Chocolate Cream (recipe follows)

In small saucepan over medium heat, stir together sugar, water and bourbon; bring to boil, stirring to dissolve sugar. Remove from heat and keep warm.

In top of double boiler over simmering water, melt chocolate; transfer to food processor. With machine running, gradually pour sugar syrup through feed tube; process until smooth. With machine running, add butter pieces, then eggs, 1 at a time. Add flour and process for 12 seconds.

Lightly grease a deep 9-inch round cake pan; line bottom with parchment or waxed paper and grease paper. Pour batter into prepared pan, running spatula over top to smooth.

Place cake pan in shallow roasting pan. Pour enough boiling water into roasting pan to come 1 inch up side of cake pan. Place roasting pan in centre of 350°F oven; bake for 50 to 60 minutes or until top forms thin, dry crust like a brownie. Remove cake pan from water bath, wipe dry and let cool.

Invert onto flat plate, peel off parchment, and quickly but gently invert onto serving plate (cake may settle at this point) Mound centre of cake with white chocolate curls and sprinkle with chocolate curls.

TO SERVE: Place thin slices of cake on dessert plates with a dollop of White Chocolate Cream. *Serves 10 to 12.*

12	oz white chocolate, finely chopped
1	cup 35% cream
2	tbsp bourbon
2	tbsp Kirsch

White Chocolate Cream

In top of double boiler over simmering water, melt chocolate. In small saucepan, heat cream until scalding; whisk into chocolate, stirring until smooth. Stir in bourbon and Kirsch. Transfer cream mixture to container with tight-fitting lid and refrigerate overnight. Let come to room temperature before using. *Makes 2 cups.*

FRANGELICO MOUSSE WITH CHAMPAGNE SABAYON

THE COUNTRY SQUIRE, NARAMATA, BC / *Owner/Chef: Patt Dyck*

The flavour of this melt-in-your-mouth dessert is best described as "heavenly." The mousse is prepared one day in advance, whereas the romantic Champagne Sabayon is prepared just before serving to ensure its light texture.

1 1/3	cups hazelnuts
4	egg yolks
2/3	cup granulated sugar
1	tsp vanilla extract
1/3	cup Frangelico
1 1/2	cups 35% cream
	Champagne Sabayon (recipe follows)

On baking sheet, toast hazelnuts in 350°F oven for 10 to 15 minutes or until golden. Remove from oven; immediately wrap nuts in tea towel and let steam for 15 minutes. Rub vigorously to remove skins; let cool. Set aside 1/3 cup of the nuts for garnish. In food processor, grind remaining nuts until fine. Set aside.

With mixer, beat together egg yolks, sugar and vanilla until thickened and lemon-coloured. Fold in nuts and Frangelico.

With mixer and clean bowl, beat cream until stiff peaks form; stir half into nut mixture. Fold in remaining cream. Pour mousse into lightly greased 8-oz ramekins, filling two-thirds full. Freeze for about 12 hours or overnight.

TO SERVE: Briefly set each ramekin in hot water to soften slightly. Run knife around mousse and use knife to "pop" out onto dessert plates. Serve with Champagne Sabayon on the side. Garnish with reserved toasted hazelnuts. *Serves 6.*

3	egg yolks
1/4	cup granulated sugar
1/2	cup Champagne

Champagne Sabayon

In top of double boiler over simmering water, beat egg yolks and sugar until foamy and pale. Add Champagne, a little at a time, whisking constantly, until mixture begins to thicken. (Be careful not to overheat as mixture will separate.) Continue whisking until thickened and falls in ribbons. Serve immediately. *Makes 3/4 cup.*

WARM PECAN PIE WITH VANILLA BEAN ICE CREAM

THE LATCH COUNTRY INN, SIDNEY, BC / *Innkeeper: Heidi Rust*

All desserts should be a little bit sinful, and this pecan-filled pie with its warm buttery flavour fulfills that mandate. If you make the pie ahead, warm it slightly before serving with vanilla bean ice cream.

1 1/2	cups all-purpose flour
1	tbsp granulated sugar
1	tbsp vanilla custard powder*
1/3	cup room temperature butter
	ice water

Pastry

In bowl, combine flour, sugar and custard powder; add butter and mix with fingertips until mixture resembles fine crumbs. Gradually add ice water (about 4-5 tbsp) with fingertips until you can form a soft ball. Wrap in plastic wrap and refrigerate for at least 30 minutes.

On lightly floured surface, roll out dough to 1/8-inch thickness. Fit into 9-inch pie plate.

*Vanilla custard powder, a combination of cornstarch, salt and vanilla flavouring, is found in the baking section of supermarkets. Most Canadians know the product by the name Bird's Custard Powder.

1	cup brown or granulated sugar**
1	cup corn syrup
1/4	cup butter, melted
3	eggs, lightly beaten
	pinch salt
1 1/2	cups pecans
	pastry shell

Filling

In bowl, stir together sugar, corn syrup, butter, eggs and salt until well combined; mix in pecans. Pour into pastry shell. Bake in 325°F oven for 50 minutes or until golden brown. Remove from oven and let cool until warm. *Serves 8.*

**Pecan pie is traditionally made with brown sugar but you may use white (granulated) if you desire a lighter-coloured pie.

Innkeeper's wine suggestion: Mission Hill Grand Reserve Icewine (Vidal), 1997

NANAIMO BARS

KIPLING'S AT THE EMPRESS HOTEL, VICTORIA, BC / *Pastry Chef: Ken Harper*

One could not compile a recipe book of Pacific Coast flavours without including Nanaimo bars, those sweet little chocolate and cream squares that take their name from a city on the east coast of Vancouver Island. Their reputation is so far-reaching that they can be found at bake sales, afternoon teas and wedding receptions from British Columbia to Newfoundland. Nanaimo bars are a Canadian tradition, and this recipe from Kipling's at The Empress hotel shows how to prepare them perfectly.

2	cups graham cracker crumbs
1	cup sweetened coconut
1/2	cup chopped walnuts
3/4	cup + 1 tbsp butter
1/4	cup granulated sugar
5	tbsp cocoa powder
1	egg, beaten
1	tsp vanilla extract
2	cups icing sugar
3	tbsp milk
2	tbsp vanilla custard powder*
4	oz semisweet chocolate, chopped

In bowl, combine graham cracker crumbs, coconut and walnuts; set aside.

In top of double boiler over simmering water, combine 1/2 cup of the butter, sugar, cocoa, egg and vanilla; cook, stirring constantly, until mixture is thickened. Stir into crumb mixture; press into buttered 9-inch square cake pan.

With mixer, cream 1/4 cup of the remaining butter, icing sugar, milk and vanilla custard powder until light and creamy; spread over crumb base and refrigerate until hardened.

In top of double boiler over simmering water, melt chocolate and remaining butter, whisking until smooth; drizzle over top of squares. Refrigerate until firm. Cut into squares. *Makes 2 dozen.*

*Vanilla custard power, a combination of cornstarch, salt and vanilla flavouring, is found in the baking section of supermarkets. Most Canadians know the product by the name Bird's Custard Powder.

DELIGHT OF THE KING

THE TEAHOUSE RESTAURANT IN STANLEY PARK, VANCOUVER, BC / *Executive Chef: Lynda Larouche*

These spectacular swan-shaped sweets are almost too pretty to eat! Executive chef Lynda Larouche comments that they have been a favourite at The Teahouse for many years and have been a tradition with newly engaged couples. Do not be daunted by the recipe; the swans are not difficult to make.

1	cup water
1/2	cup butter
3/4	tsp + 1/2 tsp salt
1	cup all-purpose flour
4	eggs + 1 egg
1	cup 35% cream, whipped
	icing sugar
1 1/2	cups fresh berries of choice
	Chocolate Sauce (see Warm Rain Forest Crunch Banana with Hot Chocolate Sauce, page 122)

In saucepan over medium-high heat, bring water, butter and 1/2 tsp salt to boil. Remove from heat as soon as liquid boils; add flour all at once and beat vigorously with wooden spoon until mixture is smooth and pulls away from pan. Beat for 30 to 45 seconds over low heat to dry mixture. Remove from heat and let cool slightly.

Beat 1 egg and set aside. Beat 3 of the remaining eggs into warm dough, 1 at a time, beating well after each addition. Beat in just enough of the reserved egg to make very shiny mixture.

Reserve 1 cup of the dough and spoon remaining into pastry bag fitted with star #10 tip. Make swan bodies by piping 10 to 12 ovals, each about 3 x 1 1/2 inches, onto lightly greased baking sheet. Place reserved dough in pastry bag fitted with plain #3 tip. Pipe 15 S-shaped necks, each 3 to 4 inches long, on second lightly greased baking sheet (make extra necks to allow for breakage).

In small bowl, beat remaining 1 egg and remaining 1/2 tsp salt to make egg glaze; lightly brush over bodies and necks. To ensure even rising, gently press each body with back of fork dipped in cold water.

Bake in 400°F oven for 15 minutes or until necks are browned. Remove necks and transfer to racks and let cool. Bake bodies for 10 to 15 minutes longer or until browned. Transfer to racks and let cool.

TO SERVE: Cut swan bodies in half horizontally, then cut each top piece in half lengthwise to form wings. Stir berries into whipped cream; spoon cream mixture into body cavity. Insert neck in cream at 1 end of body. Place wings in cream at an angle so that they spread up and out from neck. Place swans on dessert plates; dust with icing sugar and drizzle Chocolate Sauce around swans. *Makes 10 to 12 swans.*

PROFILES

OKANAGAN VALLEY

The Okanagan Valley of British Columbia encompasses a large north-south valley positioned between vast mountain ranges to the east and west. In a province of extreme mountainous terrain, this valley is an unlikely geographical jewel, with its fertile soil, large recreational lakes and mild dry climate. Hot summer temperatures and long days of light due to its northern latitude make the Okanagan Valley one of Canada's premier fruit-farming and wine-producing areas. All the fine restaurants featured in this section seasonally adjust their menus to take full advantage of the local bounty.

THE AMPHORA BISTRO AT HAINLE VINEYARDS ESTATE WINERY

Hainle Vineyards Estate Winery is one of the province's smallest estate wineries, producing approximately 5,500 cases annually, many bearing the "British Columbia Certified Organic" label.

Food and wine naturally go together — and what better way to pair the wonderful wines of the Okanagan Valley than with foods that feature local ingredients? The Amphora Bistro opened its doors in 1995 after being granted the province's first food licence for wineries.

Winery co-owner and marketing director Sandra Hainle works closely with chef David Forestell to create a new menu each week. The restaurant has built a strong reputation, offering diners the best of local products presented in a flavourful and creative manner. Seasonal dishes may feature a starter of Smoked B.C. Sockeye Salmon on Petite Rösti Potatoes or Roasted Squash Soup with Bacon and Roasted Shallots, followed by entrées such as the creamy vegetarian Risotto Blanco with Savoy Spinach and Sweet Peas or the delicate Roasted Chicken with Sautéed Endive, Yellow Finn Potatoes and Yellow Tomatoes. If your appetite allows, you may want to finish your repast with Ricotta Cassata with Fruit and Chocolate or Warm Walnut Bread Pudding with Caramelized Apples and Vanilla Bean Ice Cream.

The bistro offers on-site and off-site catering, custom dinners and cooking classes that feature chef Forestell and other prominent Canadian chefs. In conjunction with Hainle Vineyards, the bistro produces a quarterly newsletter filled with food and wine information.

5355 Trepanier Bench Road
Peachland, BC V0H 1X0
Telephone: (250) 767-2525 or 1-800-767-3109
Fax: (250) 767-2543
Web site: www.hainle.com

Open April through October
Lunch: Tuesday through Sunday and holiday Mondays
Restaurateur: Sandra Hainle • Executive Chef: David Forestell

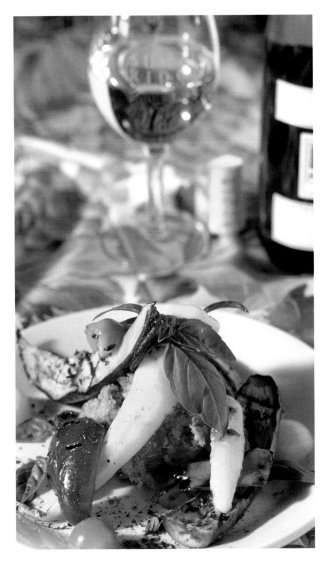

savoury appetizers, soups, vegetarian specialties and main courses are simply prepared yet rich with intense flavours.

During off-season winter months, join Reinhardt and Taylor at their new J.R.'s Restaurant located in Sheeprock Lodge, at the Apex Mountain Resort near Penticton.

Located at Sumac Ridge Estate Winery
P.O. Box 566
17403 Highway 97 North
Summerland, BC   V0H 1Z0
Telephone: (250) 494-3316 Fax: (250) 494-3456
Web site: www.vip.net/cdbistro

Open May to early November • Lunch and dinner daily
Catering service: in main dining room and off premises,
in-season and off-season
Owners: Mark Taylor and Dana Reinhardt

CELLAR DOOR BISTRO & CATERING

Husband and wife team Dana Reinhardt and Mark Taylor lease space at Sumac Ridge Estate Winery to operate their popular Cellar Door Bistro. Taylor manages the restaurant while Reinhardt prepares the cuisine. The bistro shares space with the winery's wine shop and tasting centre in a building atop a knoll within the winery complex. There is a bustle of lively activity as each business operates separately yet symbiotically.

Reinhardt takes full advantage of the businesses' relationship in her expert execution of dishes that complement and enhance the wines and produce of the region. The restaurant's menu changes seasonally to accommodate the best local products.

The atmosphere at Cellar Door Bistro is fresh yet warm and relaxed, with its peach-coloured walls, large stone fireplace and expansive windows that let in the Okanagan sunshine. A variety of fresh organic salads,

THE COUNTRY SQUIRE

Owners Patt and Ron Dyck of The Country Squire must rely on their reputation to draw patrons as one would never just "happen" upon their establishment. The restaurant is nestled in the little village of Naramata, off the beaten track on the quiet side of Lake Okanagan.

In the early 1900s the area was bustling with commerce and the rail and boat traffic it drew. Today the prosperity of the region lies in the desert-like soil that comes alive with irrigation. Driving from Penticton to Naramata one passes many fruit farms and vineyards that spread up from the lakeshore to the rising hills.

The produce from these farms and the wines from the vineyards inspire chef Patt Dyck to create the wonderful menus that keep her customers coming back. The dimly lit dining rooms invite a full evening of fine dining, relaxation and conversation. According to Dyck, most guests take a stroll along the shore between courses.

Nightly sittings begin at 6 p.m. and feature eight varied entrées, along with Dyck's superbly prepared soups, salads, breads and desserts. All dishes are prepared in the restaurant's kitchen with the choicest of local products.

3950 First Street
Naramata, BC   V0H 1N0
Telephone: (250) 496-5416
Web site: www.country-squire.com

Open year-round • Dinner: Thursday through Sunday • Reservations required
Owners: Patt and Ron Dyck

DE MONTREUIL

Situated in the heart of downtown Kelowna, de Montreuil is an unpretentious light, bright restaurant that exudes an easy, relaxed atmosphere. Brothers Grant and Michael de Montreuil opened the restaurant in 1995 and have built a solid reputation for serving creative West Coast cuisine.

On the menu you will find an array of dishes that feature fresh produce and meats from the Okanagan Valley and foothills of the Cascade Mountains, as well as Pacific coast seafood delivered fresh from Vancouver. Careful presentation and a masterful use of ingredients enhance, but never overwhelm, the meal.

368 Bernard Avenue
Kelowna, BC   V1Y 6N5
Telephone: (250) 860-5508 Fax: (250) 860-2715

Open year-round • Dinner: Daily • Lunch: Monday to Friday • Brunch: Sunday
Restaurateurs: Grant and Michael de Montreuil

THE HISTORIC 1912 RESTAURANT AND COUNTRY INN

Located in the little village of Kaleden, The Historic 1912 Restaurant and Country Inn is set in the original David Lapsley General Store. When one walks through the entrance, it is obvious that owners Allan and Donna Dell have recaptured, in an eclectic style, the atmosphere of a typical period general store. Collections of early 1900s memorabilia adorn the shelves, tables and floor. There is an impressive collection of photos depicting a Kaleden of days gone by. Nearly a hundred years of memories lie captured between the embossed metal ceiling and well-mellowed hardwood floors.

Meals are served in the historic dining room, in the sunroom and, during summer months, in the garden. The Dells enjoy experimenting with traditional recipes, preparing and complementing them with local produce and wines. The Scallop and Prawn Sauté entrée contains local Sumac Ridge Gewürztraminer wine and fresh orchard Bartlett pears. The Escargots en Croûtes features delicious escargots baked under a puff pastry and wild British Columbia mushrooms. The baby back ribs are marinated in a barbeque sauce made with local Tin Whistle Dark Ale.

Flower gardens cascade from the restaurant to the shores of Lake Skaha, inviting patrons to rest a while and enjoy the beauty. The restaurant features special theme dinners, monthly winemaster's dinners and a variety of bed-and-breakfast packages. Accommodation is offered in three bed-and-breakfast suites located above the restaurant and in a one-bedroom guesthouse.

100 Alder Avenue
Kaleden, BC   V0H 1K0
Telephone: (250) 497-6868 or 1-888-633-1912
Fax: (250) 497-6813
Web site: www.1912.com

Open from Easter until Christmas
Dinner daily
Proprietors: Allan and Donna Dell

SALTY'S BEACH HOUSE RESTAURANT

You would expect to find Salty's Beach House Restaurant under swaying palm trees on some exotic isle. Though it's definitely located on the beach, the beach happens to be in the town of Penticton on the shores of Lake Okanagan. Owner Robert Wylie reveals his wry sense of humour as he takes patrons on a seafaring "cook's tour" of the world. Salty's offers a taste of saltier climes with its funky beach-bum decor, laid-back Caribbean music and delicious seafood.

On the menu are an international selection of soups, salads, entrées, wood-fired pizzas and desserts, all prepared with fresh local ingredients. Menu items prefaced by a palm tree symbol indicate health-conscious dishes.

Salty's, known by locals and visitors as a fun dining spot with exceptional food, is listed in Anne Hardy's *Where to Eat in Canada* restaurant guide.

1000 Lakeshore Drive
Penticton, BC   V2A 1C1
Telephone: (250) 493-5001 Fax: (250) 493-8400

Mid-May to mid-October: Lunch and dinner daily
Mid-October to mid-May: Dinner daily
Owner: Robert Wylie

SMOKEHAUS VERANDA RESTAURANT AT SUMMERHILL ESTATE WINERY

Summerhill Estate Winery, the largest certified organic vineyard in Canada, is situated high on a steep hillside overlooking the city of Kelowna. On a clear sunny day the stunning vista from the winery's aptly named Smokehaus Veranda Restaurant encompasses more than 40 kilometres of Lake Okanagan.

There is much to see and do at Summerhill: take a tour of the only "Champagne"–making facility in Canada, wonder at the Great Pyramid replica used to age the award-winning wines, enjoy free wine tastings, or browse through the gift and wine shop.

Of course, it is essential that you experience lunch or sushi and hors d'oeuvres in the winery's veranda-style restaurant during your visit. Chef Graham Pierce offers delicious soups, salads, desserts, expertly prepared entrées and his famous Smoked Salmon Eggs Benedict for luncheon guests. Many of these dishes feature ingredients smoked on the premises, and all are designed to complement Summerhill wines. Late afternoon and early evening fare includes small appetizers and authentic Japanese sushi. As well, the restaurant offers catered dinners for special events.

Owner Stephen Cipes' vision is "to provide the very best from pure nature for those who appreciate all natural foods and wines."

4870 Chute Lake Road
Kelowna, BC   V1W 4M3
Telephone: (250) 464-8000 Fax: (250) 764-2598
Web site: www.summerhill.bc.ca

Open year-round • Lunch: 11:00 a.m. to 3:00 p.m.
Sushi and hors d'oeuvres: 3:00 to 7:00 p.m. daily
Winemaker/Owner: Stephen Cipes • Chef: Graham Pierce

WHITE CRYSTAL INN RESTAURANT & LOUNGE

It takes only a cursory glance at the horizon to realize that even though you may be nestled in the moderate dry climate of the Okanagan Valley, the mountains with their winter wonderland are always close at hand. Drive forty-five minutes east from the city of Kelowna and you will find Big White, the Okanagan Valley's largest ski area with a vertical of 2,550 feet.

The White Crystal Inn Restaurant & Lounge is located slopeside in the White Crystal Inn. Winner of the 1998/99 Best Accommodation Award at Big White, the inn offers fifty deluxe rooms, many with kitchenettes and gas fire-

places. The colourfully decorated restaurant features a large fireplace conducive to after-ski relaxation. Full buffet breakfasts, casual healthy lunches and refined evening dining are offered to inn guests and the general public.

Co-owner/chef Helmut Pflueger's seasonal menus offer delicious cuisine prepared with local ingredients; according to Pflueger, "local" in the Big White area may mean Alaska, the northwest U.S.A. or the western provinces of Canada. He feels that good ingredients are the essence of fine food — more important than profound culinary ideas or masterful techniques. On the menu you will find fresh soups and seafood and meat entrées, with complimentary salad bar and desserts.

5229 Big White Road, Big White, BC
Mailing address:
P.O. Box 2006, Station R
Kelowna, BC   V1X 4K5
Telephone: Inn reservations (250) 765-4611
Restaurant reservations, (250) 491-1396
Central reservation booking agency: 1-800-663-2772
Web site: www.bigwhite.com

Open year-round • Breakfast, lunch and dinner daily
Restaurateurs: Helmut Pflueger, Jari and Dasa Nydr

VANCOUVER AND ENVIRONS

Celebrated as one of the world's most beautiful cities, Vancouver is a visitor's dream destination and resident's ideal home. Known as Canada's Gateway to the Pacific, the city takes pride in its international character and wealth of cultural and natural entertainment. The Vancouver dining scene is considered to be among the finest in the world, with a variety of first-class restaurants featuring traditional, ethnic, contemporary Pacific Northwest and fusion-style cuisine.

BEACH SIDE CAFÉ

Located on Vancouver's north shore, Beach Side Café overlooks the Ambleside Sailing Club and beach. The restaurant features a main dining room on two levels: an intimate candle-lit wine cellar for small group dinners and a patio deck. In summer, the second-storey patio offers diners an ever-changing vista of harbour activity. The ambience at Beach Side Café is friendly and bright, with efficient service.

Executive chef Carol Chow, well known in Vancouver culinary circles, offers patrons contemporary Pacific Northwest cuisine simply and impeccably prepared. Her menu changes frequently to harmonize with seasonal ingredients. It is chef Chow's intention "to let the ingredients speak for themselves." The wine list, carefully chosen to accent menu items, is managed by sommelier Mark Davidson.

1362 Marine Drive
West Vancouver, BC V7T 1B5
Telephone: (604) 925-1945 Fax: (604) 925-1202

Open year-round • Dinner: Daily • Lunch: Monday to Saturday
Brunch: Sunday • Owner: Janet McGuire • Executive Chef: Carol Chow

BIN 941 TAPAS PARLOUR

Chef and owner Gordon Martin has successfully brought to the Vancouver dining scene his upscale version of Iberian tapas dining. Tapas, or "little snacks," are traditionally served in small specialty bars. Like the atmosphere in European counterparts, BIN 941 is eclectic, social and hopping with activity.

BIN 941 Tapas Parlour is popular and very small (seating for thirty), so be prepared to come early or wait in line. The restaurant features an open kitchen with banquette-style, bar and kitchen-counter seating. Martin has fused traditional Old World tapas selections with his own blend of Pacific Northwest cuisine. The resulting flavours are complex, at times exotic, and always good. Among the menu items are a southern-styled Cinnamon Chili Rub Texas Flank Steak with Maple Syrup Chipotle Glaze and Black Pepper Pommes Frites, East West Crab Cakes with Burnt Orange Chipotle Sauce and Charred Baby Bok Choy, and four globe-spanning variations of fresh mussels. An extensive selection of wines and handcrafted beers, chosen to highlight the cuisine, are served from the bar.

The success of BIN 941 has encouraged Martin to open a second establishment, not surprisingly named BIN 942, at 1521 West Broadway (at Granville Street). BIN 942 is open for lunch Monday to Friday, and for dinner daily from 5 p.m. to late night.

941 Davie Street (at Burrard Street)
Vancouver, BC   V6Z 1B9
Telephone: (604) 683-1246 Fax: (604) 683-1206

Open year-round • Lunch: Tuesday to Friday
Dinner: Tuesday, Wednesday and Sunday, 5:30 p.m. to midnight
Thursday, Friday and Saturday, 5:30 p.m. to 2:00 a.m.
Closed Monday • Owner/Executive Chef: Gordon Martin

BISHOP'S RESTAURANT

John Bishop, the delightfully warm and inviting owner of Bishop's, describes his restaurant's culinary style as "international new food." By combining traditional European cooking techniques with the large variety of fresh interna-

tional ingredients available in the Vancouver marketplace, he and his staff are able to create fare that keeps faithful patrons coming back. Under the direction of executive chef Dennis Green, the menu is changed (at times even daily) to accommodate fresh seasonal products. Always included are specialties such as rack of lamb, fresh seafood and fillet of beef. All dishes are prepared on site, including fresh-baked bread, pastries and desserts.

Bishop's, with its efficient and casually elegant dining room, is located on bustling West Fourth Avenue in the Kitsilano district and is open daily for dinner.

2183 West Fourth Avenue
Vancouver, BC   V6K 1N7
Telephone: (604) 738-2025 Fax: (604) 738-4622
Web site: www.bishops.net

Open year-round • Dinner daily
Owner: John Bishop • Executive Chef: Dennis Green

BORGO ANTICO RISTORANTE

In the late 1960s the city of Vancouver embarked on a plan to reclaim Gastown — one of the most historical, yet rundown, areas of the city — named after Vancouver's founding father "Gassy Jack Deighton." The original transformation successfully brought new life to the old cobblestone sidewalks, streets and quaint little storefronts. Most recently Gastown is being transformed with the remodelling of many Victorian buildings into trendy loft-style living quarters and workspaces. This is a wonderful area to experience the Vancouver of old. You may browse through small antique shops and galleries, stop to sample the produce and flowers of local vendors or relax over a lingering lunch or dinner.

Italians love to wine, dine and socialize and their greatest delight is in sharing that experience with everyone. Umberto Menghi, owner of Borgo Antico

Ristorante, located in the heart of Gastown at 321 Water Street, invites patrons to pass through the iron-gated entrance into a world of culinary excitement. The restaurant offers dining on the terrace, in the main dining room, in the upstairs area and in the wine room. You may choose an atmosphere to suit your mood: open and bustling or secluded and quiet. The menu features traditional Mediterranean-style cuisine utilizing the finest meats, seafood and produce. Choose from a wide variety of appetizers, soups, salads, pastas, risotto, main courses and desserts. Borgo Antico has an extensive international selection of wines.

321 Water Street
Vancouver, BC   V6B 1B8
Telephone: (604) 683-8376
Web site: www.umberto.com

Open year-round • Lunch and Dinner: Monday to Saturday
Closed Sundays and holidays • Owner: Umberto Menghi

C RESTAURANT

In a few short years, Harry Kambolis has created the definitive seafood restaurant catering to avant-garde gourmand tastes. Situated on the busy waterfront at Falsecreek, C Restaurant is the epitome of modernity. The two-storey restaurant features vaulted ceilings and expansive viewing windows that overlook a profusion of water activity. Simple, chic, cool, and classy all describe the ambience of C. Whether they are on the busy main level, seated in high-backed chairs surrounding tables dressed in crisp white-linen or in the more intimate upstairs gallery, diners experience the cutting edge of style and cuisine.

Seafood, impeccably prepared and presented as a work of art, is the main focus of the menu. For those inclined toward meat or vegetarian entrées, there is an equally delectable section on the menu entitled "Also

Available." You may choose from several varieties of caviar at the raw seafood bar as well as a host of appetizers, main courses, and desserts. A fixed price sampler menu featuring six courses plus dessert is an excellent way to experience the true talents of chef de cuisine Rob Clarke and his kitchen staff. A comprehensive wine list features an international selection of fine wines served by the glass or bottle.

2-1600 Howe Street (on Falsecreek Waterfront)
Vancouver, BC   V6Z 2L9
Telephone: (604) 681-1164 Fax: (604) 605-8263
Web site: www.crestaurant.com

Open year-round • Lunch: Sunday to Friday • Dinner: Daily
Restaurateur: Harry Kambolis • Chef de Cuisine: Rob Clarke

CIN CIN

When you dine at Cin Cin you feel all the sun-splashed warmth of the Mediterranean countryside. A spirit of mellow gaiety infuses the decor and atmosphere. The restaurant more than measures up to its quaint name, derived from chin chin, a toast meaning "to good health, old friends and the pleasures of food and wine."

Situated in the heart of busy downtown Vancouver, upstairs at 1154 Robson Street, Cin Cin offers French- and Italian-style fare augmented by premier local ingredients. Here you will find specialties from the restaurant's alder-fired oven, grill and rotisserie, including Wood Oven-Baked Artichoke Hearts with Bell Peppers, Onions, Garlic Mayonnaise and Nicoise Olives, Halibut Steak on the Bone with Traditional Vegetable Ratatouille and Sea Urchin Roe Sauce, and Pizza with Mushrooms and Nechako Valley Goat Cheese. For those who prefer a meatless entrée, a comprehensive vegetarian menu is offered daily.

All baked goods are prepared on site, including an

exciting variety of sumptuous desserts. As well, Cin Cin offers an extensive wine selection carefully selected to accentuate the cuisine.

1154 Robson Street (2nd floor)
Vancouver, BC V6E 1B5
Telephone: (604) 688-7338 Fax: (604) 688-7339
Web site: www.cincin.net

Open year-round • Lunch: Monday to Friday
Dinner: Daily • Mid-afternoon and late-night menu available
Executive Chef: Romy Prasad • Owner: Jack Evrensel

DIVA AT THE MET

Diva at the Met, located in the luxurious Metropolitan Hotel in downtown Vancouver's business district, is much more than your standard hotel restaurant. Expectations run high when you dine at Diva because Michael Noble, internationally renowned Canadian Chef of the Year for 1999, oversees the running of the kitchen. You will not be disappointed, for chef Noble lives up to his reputation, ingeniously creating his own brand of international cuisine using British Columbian ingredients interwoven with the eclectic culinary styles of other countries. Enjoy dishes such as Deep Water Oysters with Melon Sunomono and Cucumber Water, Pan-Seared Wild Chinook Salmon with Dungeness Crab and Fennel Broth, and Potato-Crusted Loin of Lamb "Iron Chef." (The latter is named after the popular Japanese competitive cooking show, "Iron Chef," on which chef Noble made an appearance.) Noble's mastery of the balance of flavour, texture and presentation is quite evident in the dessert Stilton Cheesecake with Rhubarb Compote, which received GQ Magazine's Top Taste Award for 1997.

Diva at the Met is superbly decorated in neutral shades, highlighted with glass, marble and bronze to produce a natural warm effect. A centrally located Waldorf-style open kitchen affords patrons interesting views of

food preparation. The service is impeccable; the attentive, informed staff make your dining experience memorable. Diva at the Met is open for breakfast, lunch, weekend brunch, dinner and after-theatre dining.

The Metropolitan Hotel is designated an AAA four-diamond hotel and is a member of the luxury collection of Preferred Hotels & Resorts Worldwide. The hotel was originally constructed according to the ancient Chinese art of feng shui and continues in that tradition today. Hotel amenities include 197 deluxe guest rooms and suites, health club and spa, conference and private dining services, catering service and an executive business centre complete with secretarial service and all office amenities.

645 Howe Street
Vancouver, BC   V6C 2Y9
Restaurant telephone: (604) 602-7788
Restaurant fax: (604) 643-7267
Hotel reservations: (604) 687-1122
or 1-800-667-2300
Hotel fax: (604) 689-7044
Web site: www.metropolitan.com

Open year-round
Breakfast, lunch, dinner and after-theatre dining daily • Weekend brunch
Hotel Manager: Jeremy Roncoroni • Executive Chef: Michael Noble

IL GIARDINO AND UMBERTO'S

Owner Umberto Menghi divides his time between his empire of five acclaimed Vancouver and Whistler area restaurants and his Villa Delia Cooking School, in the beautiful rolling hills of Tuscany. He is in the enviable position of bringing culinary joy to all who love to eat and prepare Italian-style cuisine. Each of his restaurants features a slightly different ambience, and four of them offer a different menu. All can be counted on to provide a memorable meal of fine food, fine wine and superb service.

Il Giardino and Umberto Menghi's original restaurant,

Umberto's, located next door, maintain separate exteriors but are accessible to each other on the inside and share a common kitchen and menu. Umberto's, the smaller of the two establishments, offers dining for small groups, while Il Giardino, designed after a Tuscan home, offers seating in the main dining room and patio.

The only problem you will encounter at Il Giardino and Umberto's is deciding what to order. The extensive menu and wonderful aromas wafting from the kitchen make the decision almost unbearable. Will you sample Carousel of Antipasti savour Grilled Assorted Mushroom's and Roasted Garlic, or sup on traditional Minestrone Vegetable Soup? Will you try a pasta such as Cannelloni Filled with Game Meats or choose an entrée such as Ossobuco Milanese with Saffron Risotto? Whatever you decide, you will not be disappointed.

1382 Hornby Street
Vancouver, BC   V6Z 1W5
Telephone: (604) 669-2422
Web site: www.umberto.com

Open year-round
Lunch: Monday to Friday, from 12:00 p.m. • Dinner: Daily from 5:30 p.m.
Owner: Umberto Menghi

LE CROCODILE

Vancouver is a city with sophisticated tastes. Diners know what they like and how it should be prepared. It is evident that owner/chef Michel Jacob must be preparing his Alsace-style French cuisine perfectly at Le Crocodile for he has remained high on diners' and critics' lists since the restaurant's inception in 1983. Chef Jacob and his staff take pride in using authentic French culinary techniques to create all their own stocks, sauces and accompaniments from the finest products available.

In stylishly elegant surroundings, you will be served traditional French dishes such as Alsacian-Style Onion Tart and Curly Endive Salad, Pan-Fried Dover Sole with Beurre Noisette and Capers, and French Lemon Tart. The fine selection of wines and spirits were chosen to enhance the menu.

100-909 Burrard Street
Vancouver, BC   V6Z 2N2
Telephone: (604) 669-4298 Fax: (604) 669-4207

Open year-round • Lunch: Monday to Friday • Dinner: Monday to Saturday
Closed Sunday • Owner/Chef: Michel Jacob

ORITALIA

Oritalia, modelled after the successful Oritalia Restaurant in San Francisco, opened its Vancouver doors in April 1999. Located at 567 Hornby Street, adjacent to Le Soleil Sheraton Hotel in the downtown business district, Oritalia is a vivacious restaurant complete with open kitchen. The decor, with its accents of gold and red, expresses a unique fusion of European and Asian styles. Meals are served in the busy downstairs main dining room and intimate upstairs area, and in the private dining room for group gatherings.

Under the direction of executive chef Julian Bond, the kitchen creates fare that successfully reflects the restaurant's fusion-style atmosphere. Thai Curry Beef with Ginger Aïoli, Avocado and Hearts of Romaine, Nori-Wrapped Dungeness Crab Cakes with Lemongrass Cream, and Orange Cardamom French Toast feature a marriage of Mediterranean and Asian Pacific cuisine. Oritalia begins serving breakfast at 6:30 a.m. followed by lunch, dinner and late-night dining.

567 Hornby Street
Vancouver, BC   V6C 2E8
Telephone: (604) 689-8862 Fax: (604) 689-8867

Open year-round • Breakfast daily from 6:30 a.m.
Lunch daily from 11:00 a.m. • Dinner daily from 5:00 p.m.
Late-night menu daily from 11:00 p.m.
Restaurateurs: Bob Puccini and "Taisho" M. Nori Yoshido
Executive Chef: Julian Bond

Web site: www.cyberpathway.com/seasons

Open year-round • Lunch, dinner and weekend brunch
Management: Sequoia Enterprises Inc. • Executive Chef: Pierre Delacote

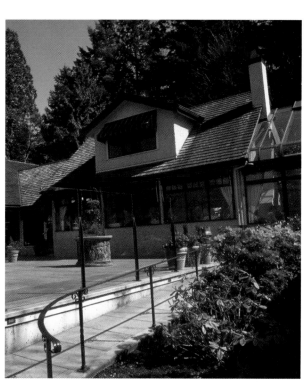

SEASONS RESTAURANT IN QUEEN ELIZABETH PARK

Seasons Restaurant is situated in Queen Elizabeth Park
on a knoll that is the highest promontory within
Vancouver's city limits. Reclaimed from two spent rock
quarries, the park, with its beautiful gardens and streams,
is a tribute to the environmental consciousness of British
Columbians. With its expansive windows and skylights,
Seasons Restaurant offers diners an atmosphere of airy
brightness that is complementary to the park-like surroundings. During the day, diners delight in a stunning
vista of manicured gardens and parkland spreading out to
the big city skyline and mountains beyond. At night, candle-lit tables sparkle in competition with the lights of the
city below. The decor is comfortable and relaxing, with
neutral-coloured woods, crisp white linens and greenery.

Executive chef Pierre Delacote prepares traditional
continental cuisine enhanced by regional ingredients.
Menu highlights include Smoked Alaskan Black Cod
with Grainy Mustard Beurre Blanc, Shallot and Green
Apple–Stuffed Maple-Roasted Free-Range Chicken and
chef Delacote's signature Sunburnt Lemon Pie.

Little Mountain in Queen Elizabeth Park
Cambie Street at 33rd Street
Vancouver, BC
Mailing Address:
1583 Coal Harbour Quay
Vancouver, BC   V6G 3E7
Telephone: (604) 874-8008 or 1-800-632-9422
Fax: (604) 874-7101

THE TEAHOUSE RESTAURANT IN STANLEY PARK

When you ask a Vancouverite to name the most important feature of the city, the answer is likely to be Stanley
Park. This 1,000-acre nature's wonderland was dedicated
in 1889 by Queen Victoria's Canadian representative Lord
Stanley. A pedestrian seawall and walkway, open for jog-
ging, in-line skating, walking and biking, offers spectacular views of the north shore mountains, Burrard Inlet,
English Bay and the Gulf Islands. Stroll a myriad of wind-
ing paths amid lush flora and towering Douglas fir or, if
less energetic, take a horse-drawn carriage or shuttle bus
tour. Also located within the park are the Vancouver
Aquarium and Marine Science Centre, Lost Lagoon,
Children's Zoo, rose gardens, beaches and numerous pic-
nic areas.

There is no doubt that The Teahouse Restaurant is
situated in one of the most enviable locations in
Vancouver. Originally a Second World War garrison and
officer's mess, the restaurant is nestled under a canopy of
enormous Douglas fir trees, surrounded by manicured
gardens and blessed with a view that one can imagine

leads to the Orient.

Executive chef Lynda Larouche prepares a style of contemporary West Coast cuisine that takes full advantage of the wide variety of ingredients available. "We are lucky to be in a port city where you can just about get every ingredient and spice to implement foods from across the continent and around the world," she says. Entrée specialties include Salmon Tournedos, Asian Roast Duck and Mille Feuille of Vegetables and Mushroom Sacchetti.

The Teahouse Restaurant in Stanley Park is consistently rated one of Vancouver's top restaurants, with recognition from *Gourmet, Vancouver* and *Where Vancouver* magazines, *Zagat Survey-Vancouver Restaurants 2000*, and *Fodor's Vancouver Guide*.

7501 Stanley Park Drive
Ferguson Point in Stanley Park
Vancouver, BC   V6G 3E2
Telephone: (604) 669-3281 Fax: (604) 687-5662
Web site: www.cyberpathway.com/teahouse

Open year-round • Lunch, dinner and weekend brunch
Owner: Sequoia Enterprises Inc. • Executive Chef: Lynda Larouche

TOJO'S RESTAURANT

Tojo's Restaurant may be tucked away on the second floor of a modern office tower on West Broadway but the restaurant is anything but ordinary. In fact, in a city with very high Japanese culinary standards, Tojo's is known to be "one of the best." It is a tribute to Hidekazu Tojo's talent and success that he is as highly regarded by peers in the food industry as he is by his patrons.

The restaurant is tranquilly decorated in traditional Japanese style. Seated at the sushi bar, one can focus on the intricate art form of sushi preparation and presentation; seated at a table, one can enjoy a spectacular view of the city and north shore mountains.

Consistently rated by travel and dining publications as one of Vancouver's best restaurants, Tojo's is a must for earnest sushi lovers. The menu changes regularly to take advantage of the best seasonal ingredients. Be sure to try Hidekazu Tojo's whimsically named Good Night Salmon or his Great Canadian Roll — a culinary variation on our national motto, "From Sea to Sea" — in which succulent Atlantic lobster is paired with mildly smoked Pacific salmon.

#202-777 West Broadway
Vancouver, BC   V5Z 4J7
Telephone: (604) 872-8050; 872-5051
Fax: (604) 872-8060

Open year-round • Dinner: Monday to Saturday
Owner/Restaurateur: Hidekazu Tojo

VICTORIA AND THE ISLANDS

You are never very far from the ocean and its slower pace of life when you are in Victoria and the islands. The area is blessed with a mild climate, great beauty and abundant natural and cultural activities. Here you can expect excellent cuisine and genuine hospitality.

THE AERIE RESORT

Eagles always build their aeries (nests) on the highest possible vantage point to keep a sharp eye on prey and predators. With this in mind, it is hard to imagine a more appropriate name for The Aerie Resort, perched high upon a mountainside overlooking Finlayson Arm, only a short thirty-minute drive from the city of Victoria. Opened in 1991, the Aerie Resort is a member of the elite international hotel association Relais & Châteaux, holder of both the AAA Four Diamond Award and the Mobil Four Star Award, as well as a member of the prestigious dining associations: Chaîne des Rotisseurs and Confrérie du Sabre d'Or.

The Aerie offers all the amenities of a world-class luxury resort, including an Aveda Beauty & Wellness Centre, full-service meeting facility for small- to medium-size groups, indoor roof-top pool, hot tub and sauna, outdoor hot tub and tennis court. Available nearby are a wealth of outdoor activities, including golf, kayaking, hiking, bird watching and sailing. Management will also arrange cultural, historical and winery tours for guests. Accommodation with breakfast is offered in twenty-three elegantly appointed hotel rooms and suites, many with private balconies, Jacuzzis and fireplaces.

The restaurant, under the expert direction of executive chef Chris Jones, offers resort guests and the public classic French-style cuisine showcasing Vancouver Island ingredients. "At the Aerie our recipes are never static," says Jones. "We change and suit our dishes to highlight local seasonal ingredients."

P.O. Box 108
600 Ebedora Lane
Malahat, BC V0R 2L0
Telephone: (250) 743-7115 or 1-800-518-1933   Fax: (250) 743-4766
Web site: www.aerie.bc.ca

Open year-round • Breakfast, lunch and dinner daily
Owner: Maria Schuster • General Manager: Markus Griesser
Executive Chef: Chris Jones

THE EMPRESS HOTEL
including
EMPRESS DINING ROOM
BENGAL LOUNGE
KIPLING'S
AFTERNOON TEA at THE EMPRESS

It is impossible to think of Victoria without conjuring up pictures of The Empress, the "grande dame" of Canadian Pacific Hotels. Located in the heart of British Columbia's capital city, The Empress has been standing guard over the inner harbour since its doors opened in 1908. Part of the original Canadian Pacific transportation dynasty, The Empress would greet guests recently disembarked from the Orient on Canadian Pacific steamships or who had made the arduous journey from Eastern Canada by rail. Today the mode of transportation may be different but the destination is the same. The Empress continues to offer guests the grandeur and elegance of a bygone era supplemented with today's modern amenities. In fact, The Empress has been including in *Condé Nast Traveler* magazine's list of top 500 hotels, resorts, spas and cruise lines.

Hotel features include 460 guest rooms, Entrée Gold floor accommodation with private concierge, two restaurants, lounge, daily afternoon tea and convention facilities. Health and fitness aficionados appreciate the health club, indoor pool, whirlpool, sauna and exercise room.

The Empress Dining Room features candle-lit dining in a relaxing atmosphere of luxury. Executive chef David Hammonds and his staff offer contemporary British Columbia cuisine that highlights the freshest seasonal products available. The restaurant has an award-winning wine list, featuring many local varieties, and an exceptional dessert selection from pastry chef Ken Harper.

In the Bengal Lounge you are offered à la carte dining as well as its famous curry buffet luncheon. The curry buffet tradition is a historical carry-over from the early days of The Empress and her Indo-Pacific British Commonwealth ties.

Kipling's restaurant offers less formal dining, with an all-day buffet and à la carte menu. Sunday brunch remains popular.

No one should visit Victoria without partaking of the queenly Victorian tradition of Afternoon Tea at The Empress. Perfectly brewed tea, poured from silver teapots, accompanies dainty tea sandwiches, pastries, fresh berries, warm scones, toasted crumpets and heavy Jersey cream. Queen Victoria herself would be right at home ordering a spot of tea!

721 Government Street
Victoria, BC   V8W 1E5
Telephone: (250) 384-8111 or 1-800-441-1414   Fax: (250) 381-4334
Web site: www.cphotels.ca

Open year-round • Breakfast, lunch, afternoon tea and dinner daily
General Manager: Ian Powell • Executive Chef: David Hammonds

GOOD LIFE BOOKSTORE CAFÉ
The little Good Life Bookstore Café in the village of Sooke claims to offer "sustenance for body and soul." The restaurant does not profess elegance but rather a relaxed atmosphere amid an eclectic collection of seasoned furniture, artwork and retail books. Seating is offered in two small dining rooms and outside on the deck when the weather is cooperative.

The heart and soul of the establishment lies in the small kitchen, from which a variety of well-prepared and creative dishes emerge. Chef and co-owner Ricardo Monteiro uses superior local ingredients to create Pacific Rim cuisine with a southern flair. The menu includes Tamarind Chipotle Scallops and Prawns, blending Asian tamarinds with smoky southern chipotle peppers, Curried Seafood Wraps, offering Indo-Asian flavours, and Smoked Salmon–Stuffed Chicken Breast in Phyllo with Sour Cherry–Ginger Glaze, highlighting Pacific salmon with fresh seasonal fruit.

2113 Otter Point Road
Sooke, BC   V0S 1N0
Telephone: (250) 642-6821

Open year-round
Winter: Lunch and dinner on weekends • Summer: Lunch and dinner daily
Co-owners: Veronica and Laurie McPherson, Ricardo Monteiro

THE GROTTO

For some people, the current interest in Pacific Rim influence on British Columbian cuisine is old news. In 1960 the Yoshida family opened The Grotto restaurant. Four decades and three generations later, the family continues to offer local residents and visitors their own successful style of fusion cuisine. Always in search of new ideas and flavours, current owner Mike Yoshida prepares classic Asian cuisine with an emphasis on quality local products. His black bean sauce highlights the lightly sautéed Grotto-Style Calamari, enhances fresh stir-frys and is used as a base flavouring for traditional steak entrées.

The Grotto is located on Stewart Avenue overlooking the water to Newcastle Island and is only minutes away from the Departure Bay Ferry Terminal. A window table ensures a view of Newcastle Channel and the busy waterfront.

1511 Stewart Avenue
Nanaimo, BC   V9S 4E3
Telephone: (250) 753-3303

Open year-round • Dinner: Tuesday through Sunday
Owner: Mike Yoshida • Chef: Dave Armour

HASTINGS HOUSE

This 30-acre estate is located on beautiful Salt Spring Island, the largest and most populated of the Gulf Islands. The island is accessible by plane or boat. Daily ferry service to Salt Spring Island operates from three terminals: Tsawwassen, just south of Vancouver, Swartz Bay, near Victoria, and Crofton, near Duncan on Vancouver Island.

Hastings House, a member of the prestigious hotel association Relais & Châteaux, offers guests superior accommodation in a peaceful, serene setting. Located in five different restored buildings, the inn has sixteen suites and one cottage, all individually decorated to express their own personal charm.

Under the direction of executive chef Marcel Kauer, guests are served gourmet cuisine featuring fresh produce from the fields, waters and gardens of the islands. In the words of the owners, "Hastings House strives to make each and every guest feel they have been invited to the home of a friend."

Upper Ganges Road
P.O. Box 1110
Salt Spring Island, BC   V8K 2S2
Telephone: (250) 537-2362 or 1-800-661-9255
Web site: www.hastingshouse.com

Open March 5 to December 29
Breakfast, lunch and dinner daily • Reservations required for public dining
Manager: Mark Gottaas • Executive Chef: Marcel Kauer

HERALD STREET CAFFE

Since its opening in 1982, the Herald Street Caffe has become the focal point for consistently fine dining in Victoria. Head chef Mark Finnigan and owner Paul Bell work diligently to maintain their reputation for fare that exceeds the norm. They offer impeccable service and outstanding wines served by the bottle or glass. For its wine service, the restaurant was awarded the Decanter Magazine/Robert Mondavi "Wine by the Glass" international Grand Award and the Award of Excellence from *Wine Spectator Magazine*.

The restaurant is casually elegant with a semi–open design concept featuring mellow golden hues accented with impressive artwork and floral arrangements. The linen-covered tables are set with sparkling tableware.

Chef Finnigan has extremely high standards and is highly skilled at combining ingredients, flavours and techniques into dishes of outstanding quality. If a recipe is not perfectly blended and complementary to the restaurant's style of cuisine, then it will not be served. Guests have a difficult time choosing from the outstanding items on the menu which include: Chanterelle-Stuffed Venison Medallions with Three Peppercorn Soy Vinaigrette, Grilled Pacific Halibut on Rice Stick Noodles in a Star Anise–Citrus Broth, and a host of wonderful homemade soups, salads and pastas. As well, all the breads, baked goods and delicious desserts are made on the premises. You are well advised to book early for reservations so as not to be disappointed.

546 Herald Street
Victoria, BC   V8W 1S6
Telephone: (250) 381-1441 Fax: (250) 381-1033
Web site: http://café-brio.com/dining/heraldstreetcaffe.htm

Open year-round • Dinner: Daily from 5:30 p.m.
Lunch: Wednesday to Saturday, 11:30 a.m. to 3:00 p.m.
Sunday brunch: 11:00 a.m. to 3:00 p.m.
Owner: Paul Bell • Head Chef: Mark Finnigan

THE LATCH COUNTRY INN

The Latch Country Inn was built in the early 1900s as a private summer retreat for Walter Nichol, the wealthy Vancouver publisher and Lieutenant-Governor of British Columbia from 1920 to 1926. Nichol requested that his architect build him a residence that utilized British Columbian wood wherever possible. The result was an impressive rustic structure, sided with bark-covered slabs of Douglas fir and balconies and porches constructed with tree trunks. The interior also features expansive wood decoration with panelled walls, wood trim and hand-carved railings. It is no wonder that the building remains strong and steadfast nearly a hundred years later.

Under the ownership of Heidi and Bernd Rust, The Latch Country Inn was extensively renovated and updated in 1995 to meet modern luxury standards. The inn offers five comfortable guest suites, all with private bath. Each suite highlights Canadian furnishings and original artwork.

Overnight guests are served breakfast. The dining room is open to the public for dinner every day except Tuesday; on Sunday, it is open for lunch and dinner. The restaurant uses local Pacific coast ingredients prepared in the European tradition. The menu offers traditional items such as Caesar salad, escargot, a variety of meat and seafood entrées, as well as a selection of lighter fare.

2328 Harbour Road
Sidney, BC   V8L 2P8
Telephone: (250) 656-6622 Fax: (250) 656-6212
Web site: www.latchinn.com

Open year-round • Continental breakfast for inn guests • Lunch: Sunday
Dinner: Wednesday through Monday from 5:00 p.m. (reservations appreciated)
Innkeepers: Heidi and Bernd Rust

THE MAHLE HOUSE RESTAURANT

Brother and sister partners Maureen Loucks and Delbert Horrocks have been successfully operating The Mahle House Restaurant in the little village of Cedar, a ten-minute drive south of Nanaimo, for the past seventeen years. Horrocks is the wine expert, selecting perfect wines to complement chef Loucks's wonderful food.

The house, built in 1904 and painted an unusual yet appealing orange colour, literally invites you turn and enter the driveway. Stroll through the enclosed English-style garden or take a peek at the new organic kitchen garden to see what ripe gourmet vegetables will be accompanying your evening meal. Step inside and you will find a decor that is casually elegant in a relaxed country setting.

Loucks prepares dishes from a menu that changes weekly to take advantage of the freshest products from the local area. She says that the rabbit, free-range chicken and venison come from down the road, while most of the herbs and vegetables come from her own garden. Her enthusiasm for fine cuisine is clearly evident in her preparation of recipes such as Smoked Gouda Cheese Soup, Braised Rabbit with Wild Mushrooms, Fresh Herbs and Mascarpone Cheese Polenta, and her Vegetarian Plate of roasted garlic and goat cheese mashed potatoes with grilled peppers, mushrooms, eggplant and zucchini on an Italian tomato sauce. It is essential that you leave room for dessert, especially if the White Chocolate Crème Brûlée and Boca Negra are on the menu.

2104 Hemer Road
Nanaimo, BC   V9X 1L8
Telephone: (250) 722-3621 Fax: (250) 722-3302
Web site: www.island.net/~mahle

Open year-round
Dinner: Wednesday through Sunday from 5:00 p.m. (reservations appreciated)
Owners: Maureen Loucks and Delbert Horrocks
Chef: Maureen Loucks

THE OLD HOUSE RESTAURANT

The Old House Restaurant is situated on the banks of the Courtenay River within the town of Courtenay in the lovely Comox Valley. This central region of Vancouver Island is blessed with an abundance of natural beauty that ranges from the high alpine areas of Mount Washington and the Forbidden Plateau down through rich farmland to the ocean shoreline.

Since The Old House Restaurant opened its doors in 1974, it has been the dining establishment of choice for local residents and visitors. The restaurant is surrounded with beautifully manicured gardens and lush green lawns that border the flowing river. Inside, you will be seated in one of four dining rooms with rough-hewn timbered walls, beamed ceilings and large stone fireplaces that exude an ambience of rustic warmth and charm. In summer, dining is also available on the patio.

The menu offers a variety of homemade West Coast dishes, including an extensive selection of steak and seafood. An on-site bakery prepares fresh bread and tantalizing desserts daily.

1760 Riverside Lane
Courtenay, BC   V9N 8C6
Telephone: (250) 338-5406 Fax: (250) 338-1134

Open year-round • Lunch and dinner daily
Restaurateur: Kevin Muir • Chef: Trevor Schneider

RAIN COAST CAFÉ

You only have to dine once at the Rain Coast Café to realize that the staff live up to their motto: "We take pride in everything we do." This informal little bistro in the village of Tofino, on the West coast of Vancouver Island, catches your attention the moment you cross the threshold. The decor is bright and airy, with bold artwork dominating one wall and eclectic music filling the air. An open kitchen offers views of food preparation complete with tantalizing aromas.

Rain Coast Café offers diners contemporary Pacific coast cuisine fused with hints of international flavours. The chef uses only the finest and freshest ingredients available, offering a variety of daily specials in addition to the standard menu, with special emphasis on unique vegetarian and vegan dishes.

The restaurant has been receiving positive attention from food connoisseurs and critics for innovative fare such as the comprehensive appetizer Thai Crab Cakes with Daikon Raita, Pickled Cucumber and Napa Cabbage Slaw, the vegetarian entrée Mediterranean Portobello Tier with Salsa Verde and Lemon Garlic Vinaigrette, and an Asian-style Indonesian Sweet Potato, Peanut and Coconut Soup. Award-winning British Columbian wines and micro-brewed beers are available to accompany your meal.

101-120 Fourth Street
Tofino, BC   V0R 2Z0
Telephone: (250) 725-2215 Fax: (250) 725-2530
Web site: www.raincoastcafe.com

Open year-round • Lunch and dinner daily
Restaurateur: Lisa Henderson • Chef de Cuisine: Mark Wrigley

SOOKE HARBOUR HOUSE

Each morning when Sinclair Philip strolls through his gardens or looks shoreward to the ocean, delightful challenges greet him. What bounty from the sea has been harvested at its prime, and which of the numerous varieties of vegetables, herbs, flowers and fruits are ready to be converted into fare for guests?

Sooke Harbour House has been garnering well-deserved national and international culinary awards and acclaim for many years, most recently *The Globe and Mail's* Best Restaurant in Canada and inclusion in *Gourmet* magazine's top twenty-five restaurants in the world. Seafood,

often exotic, is emphasized in entrées that may feature sea cucumber, wolf eel, pink singing scallops, crab, shrimp — the list is as long as the edible species found in local waters. Other meat and vegetarian entrées receive equal attention from the kitchen. As well, there is an ever-changing variety of appetizers, soups, salads and desserts. Dining at the inn is truly an experience that will remain etched in your fondest memories.

The inn features twenty-eight luxury rooms and suites, most with views of the Strait of Juan de Fuca and distant snow-capped Olympic Mountains. Each suite is named for its location. The Chef's Study is dedicated to culinary lovers, overlooks the gardens and is decorated with food lover's memorabilia. Three rooms at the top of the inn, known as The Bird's Nest, have stellar views of the ocean that ordinarily only a bird would see. All suites feature a wood-burning fireplace, comfortable sitting area, and balcony or terrace. A full breakfast and lunch are included in the room rates.

1528 Whiffen Spit Road
Sooke, BC   V0S 1N0
Telephone: (250) 642-3421 or 1-800-889-9688   Fax: (250) 642-6988
Web site: www.sookenet.com/shh

Open year-round • Breakfast and lunch for inn guests • Dinner daily
Innkeepers: Frederique and Sinclair Philip

SPINNAKERS BREWPUB & GUESTHOUSE

Spinnakers Brewpub & Guesthouse, which invites you to "drop down to the pub for a pint of...", fits in perfectly with Victoria's British-style atmosphere. The pub's location on the waterfront, with its expansive bank of windows, provides diners with an ever-changing view of harbour activity. It is difficult to focus your attention on the meal what with curious seals, float planes, water taxis, shore birds and an occasional aboriginal war canoe passing by.

Spinnakers, established in 1984, is the oldest craft brewery in British Columbia and produces a wide variety of natural lagers and conventional ales for its patrons. The brewpub features a traditional taproom for socializing, and the multi-level restaurant serves pub fare and contemporary West coast cuisine. Many of the dishes, including Hot and Sour Soup and Spinnakers Raspberry Vinaigrette with Mixed Greens, feature either Spinnakers' ales or malt vinegar in the recipe.

Accommodations, for adults only, are next door in an 1884 Victorian guesthouse. It has five period-decorated, luxury rooms with fireplaces and Jacuzzis. Complimentary breakfast is served at Spinnakers.

308 Catherine Street
Victoria, BC   V9A 3S8
Telephone: (250) 386-2739 Fax: (250) 384-3246
Web site: www.spinnakers.com

Open year-round • Breakfast, lunch and dinner daily • Owner: Paul Hadfield

THE WESLEY STREET

The Wesley Street is located in the Old City Quarter of downtown Nanaimo, a trendy area of small shops and eateries that have been reclaimed, refurbished and repainted. Owner Jennifer Rollison offers contemporary West Coast dining in an upscale chic atmosphere. The dining area is comfortably decorated in tones of pink and maroon; unique artwork adorns the walls and soft jazz fills the air.

Chef Ian Ter Veer's menu changes with the seasons, and the emphasis is on fresh local products. Diners enjoy seafood specialties such as Dungeness crab cakes, lightly grilled Fanny Bay oysters and halibut cooked to perfection. A number of vegetarian entrées are always offered,

as well as an excellent selection of meat entrées, appetizers, soups, salads and desserts. Food presentation equals the flavour, and the flavour is outstanding.

#1-321 Wesley Street
Nanaimo, BC   V9R 2T5
Telephone: (250) 753-4004 Fax: (250) 758-2888

Open year-round • Lunch and dinner daily
Owner: Jennifer Rollison • Chef: Ian Ter Veer

THE WICKANINNISH INN & POINTE RESTAURANT

Spending a few days at The Wickaninnish Inn in Tofino is a humbling back-to-nature experience. In summer, the sun shines and sparkles off the cold blue water; in win-

ter, Pacific storms pound wild surf over the rocks. All seasons bring their own special beauty to Tofino.

Situated on a point of land at the end of Chesterman Beach, the inn is surrounded on three sides by ocean and backed with giant old-growth forest on the fourth side. Wickaninnish offers forty-six guest rooms and suites, all with ocean views and private balconies. The decor is natural and rustic, with furniture created from recycled old-growth red cedar, fir or driftwood. Amenities include a full-service spa, conference and banquet facilities, and a gourmet restaurant.

The Point Restaurant offers innovative West Coast cuisine under the direction of executive chef Jim Garroway. The menu highlights fresh coastal seafood, local farm-fresh ingredients and an excellent selection of international and British Columbian wines.

Osprey Lane at Chesterman Beach
P.O. Box 250
Tofino, BC   V0R 2Z0
Telephone: (250) 725-3100 or 1-800-333-4604 Fax: (250) 725-3110
Web site: www.wickinn.com

Open year-round • Breakfast, lunch and dinner daily
Manager: Charles McDiarmid • Executive Chef: Jim Garroway

WHISTLER RESORT AREA

It is said that a region is defined by its cuisine. How true of the Whistler resort area, for not only is the scenery magnificent, the cuisine is also. Whistler is renowned as a world-class winter and summer sports mecca, and what better way to cap off a day of fun in the mountains than to sit down to a fine meal in a world-class restaurant.

ARAXI

Araxi, named for owner Jack Evrensel's wife, has been a mainstay of Whistler's culinary scene for nearly two decades. This classy restaurant, winner of numerous national and international food and wine accolades under the guidance of executive chef James Walt, features the partnering of classic French and Italian cooking techniques with regional Pacific Northwest products. The result is an epicurean delight of fine food expertly prepared and served.

Newly renovated, the restaurant features a 140-seat main dining room, lounge area, separate wine room for group dining, and outdoor summer patio and bar. The atmosphere is contemporary and chic, with mellow colours, impressive artwork and subtle romantic lighting. If you want to view the talents of Araxi's chefs, ask for a seat near the open kitchen, considerably buffered for noise with bevelled-glass surrounds. Guests may choose from an extensive liquor selection and wine list featuring over 12,000 bottles. Fifteen hundred of the bottles are kept on display in the 63°F wine refrigerator in the lounge.

Chef Walt keeps Araxi on the leading edge of dining excellence with his close attention to detail and pursuit of fine ingredients. Only the best products are used in the restaurant; fresh seafood is brought in daily from Vancouver, regional meat is used when possible, and local farmers provide cheeses, seasonal herbs, fruits and vegetables.

4222 Village Square
Whistler, BC   V0N 1B4
Telephone: (604) 932-4540 Fax: (604) 932-3348
Web site: www.araxi.com

Open year-round • Dinner daily • Lunch daily in summer
Owner: Jack Evrensel • Executive Chef: James Walt

EDGEWATER LODGE

It is difficult to imagine a setting more idyllic than that occupied by Edgewater Lodge on the northern outskirts of Whistler. The inn is surrounded by towering snow-capped mountains and borders a glacially fed green lake and river wistfully named River of Golden Dreams. You will wake up in the morning to a vista that is simply magnificent.

The retreat offers lodging with breakfast in twelve rooms, all with water-side and mountain views. Guests may enjoy the on-site spa, canoeing and kayaking activities, as well as golf at the adjacent Nicklaus North Golf Course. Other winter and summer attractions of the Whistler area are within close proximity.

The dining room overlooks the lake and mountains and is enclosed on three sides by large windows, making you feel at one with nature. Executive chef Thomas Piekarski prepares classic gourmet cuisine, often exercising his special flair for sauces. The tender venison is farm-raised at the lodge's own ranch north of Whistler, and local ingredients are featured in season.

#8841 Highway 99
P.O. Box 369
Whistler, BC   VON 1B0
Telephone: (604) 932-0688 or 1-888-870-9065
Fax: (604) 932-0686
Web site: www.edgewater-lodge.com

Open year-round • Dinner daily (reservations suggested)
Owner/Manager: Jay Symons • Executive Chef: Thomas Piekarski

LA RUA RESTAURANTE

La Rua Restaurante is situated at the base of Blackcomb Mountain in the Upper Village of Whistler. The restaurant's casual Mediterranean ambience is inspired by owner Mario Enero's Spanish background and tastes. The name Rua refers to the arched entrances in the old towns and villages of Enero's homeland, and he carries this inviting theme throughout the eatery.

The main dining room, with its terra-cotta tiled floor, crisp linens and large windows, offers a good vantage point to watch the hustle and bustle of activity at the base of the mountain. Stroll through another arch to enter the romantic Mural Dining Room, with its warm, soft colours surrounded by a painted mural wall. In summer, the restaurant opens for patio dining.

Executive chef Tim Meuhlbauer is a master at creating European cuisine with definite Pacific Northwest undertones. Dishes include Tagliatelle with Black Bean Ginger Lemon Sauce and Manis Seared Breast of Chicken; Pemberton Sheep Brie Cheese with Sun-Dried Tomatoes and Spanish Pine Nuts; and B.C. Salmon with Fresh Horseradish Crust and Lemon Balm Butter Sauce.

La Rua offers guests two extensive wine lists to choose from: a basic list of sixty wines selected for their value and harmony with the cuisine; and a second list, Reserve and Bin Ends, which features more than 250 selections of some of the world's best wines.

La Rua Restaurante has won many awards and was recently heralded as one of the top mountain resort restaurants in North America by *Snow Country* magazine.

Whistler Upper Village
4557 Blackcomb Way
P.O. Box 539
Whistler, BC   VON 1B0
Telephone: (604) 932-5011 Fax: (604) 932-2994
Web site: www.larua-restaurante.com

Open year-round • Dinner daily
Owner: Mario Enero • Executive Chef: Tim Meuhlbauer

QUATTRO AT WHISTLER

Many successful Vancouver restaurants have established offshoots in the Whistler resort area and diners familiar with the parent restaurants expect the same excellent fare and service there. They are not disappointed in Antonio Corsi's Quattro at Whistler located in Pinnacle Hotel and patterned after Corsi's well-known Quattro on fourth Avenue in the Kitsilano district of Vancouver. Both restaurants specialize in Roman and Northern Italian cuisine from Corsi's native Italy.

As you step through the doors at Quattro, warm herbal aromas from the kitchen beckon you to relax in a setting of mature dark woods, white dishes, crisp linens and sparkling glass. Executive chef Rob Parrott follows the Italian tradition of simple preparation using only the freshest, healthy products available. His aim is to let the ingredients "speak for themselves." Diners may choose from a variety of appetizers, soups, salads, pastas, meat and seafood entrées and desserts, complemented by wines from the restaurant's extensive wine list.

4319 Main Street
Whistler, BC   V0N 1B4
Telephone: (604) 905-4844 Fax: (604) 905-2440
Web site: www.quattroristorante.com

Open year-round • Dinner daily
Owner: Antonio Corsi • Executive Chef/Manager: Rob Parrott

RIM ROCK CAFÉ

Rim Rock Café is located on Route 99, the Sea to Sky Highway, just south of Whistler Village. Co-owners Bob Dawson and Rolf Gunther pride themselves on the quality of their restaurant's cuisine, which consistently earns Rim Rock reviews as one of the premier restaurants in the Whistler area. They specialize in fresh seafood expertly prepared, with sauces and accompaniments that highlight but never detract from the delicate ocean flavour. Equal attention is given to the soups, salads, meat entrées and desserts featured on the menu.

Rim Rock provides elegant dining in a warm casual setting. The atmosphere is relaxed, and expert service ensures a comfortable evening after an exhausting day of winter or summer sports. To avoid disappointment, make early reservations at this popular restaurant.

2117 Whistler Road
P.O. Box 1055
Whistler, BC   V0N 1B0
Telephone: (604) 932-5565 or 1-877-932-5589
Fax: (604) 938-1411
Web site: www.rimrockwhistler.com

Open year-round except mid-Oct to mid-Nov • Dinner daily
Chef/Owner: Rolf Gunther • Manager/Owner: Bob Dawson

TRATTORIA DI UMBERTO RESTAURANT

Trattoria di Umberto, one of two Umberto Menghi eateries in the village of Whistler, captures the essence of a true Italian trattoria. Here you can enjoy home cooking away from home in a milieu that is as comfortable as dining around the kitchen table. The eatery is warm and inviting, with its rustic-coloured walls, unique artwork, crisp white linens and heavenly aromas emanating from the kitchen.

Trattoria di Umberto is well suited to a relaxing lunch break during the day or a soothing evening meal after your day of sports excitement. The menu includes a variety of authentic Italian appetizers, soups, salads, pastas, seafood and meat entrées and daily dessert selections, all complemented by a fine selection of wines and liqueurs.

4417 Sundial Place
Whistler, BC   VON 1B0
Telephone: (604) 932-5858 Fax: (604) 932-5526
Web site: www.umberto.com

Open year-round • Lunch and dinner daily • Owner: Umberto Menghi

VAL D'ISÈRE RESTAURANT

It may seem a little presumptuous to open a restaurant under the shadow of Whistler and Blackcomb Mountains that's named after a famous peak in the French Alps. But owner Roland Pfaff can be forgiven for he brings us more than a name — he also shares with us his wonderful French cuisine. It is easy to see that Pfaff enjoys life and food and that his main goal is to create something special for his guests. Val d'Isère is situated in the heart of Whistler's buzzing Town Plaza and is a great spot to "people watch."

Pfaff cooks in the traditional French manner but is not averse to creating unique cuisine with the addition of local specialties. His Roast of Veal Tenderloin is accompanied by a sauce of Vancouver Island morel mushrooms, and he creates a delicious Dungeness Crab Ravioli Gratin with Smoked Salmon Sauce using local seafood. Make sure you leave room for Val d'Isère's famous desserts, such as Warm Chocolate Orange Gâteau with Voluptuous Oozing Chocolate Sauce and Iced Lemon Soufflé with Hazelnut Meringue. The wine list is extensive and well chosen to accent the cuisine.

Bear Lodge at the Town Plaza, P.O. Box 1083
Whistler, BC   VON 1B0
Telephone: (604) 932-4666 Fax: (604) 932-2186
Web site: www.valdiser@direct.ca

Open year-round • Lunch and dinner: June to mid-October daily
Dinner: Mid-October to June daily • Owner/Chef: Roland Pfaff

THE WILDFLOWER RESTAURANT AT CP CHATEAU WHISTLER RESORT

Chateau Whistler Resort, a massive stone structure featuring 558 guest rooms and suites, is located at the base of Blackcomb and Whistler Mountains. The modern château-style hotel, part of the Canadian Pacific Hotel chain, is the only one of that style to be built by the company in the past 100 years. Chateau Whistler has won numerous awards from international winter sports and travel magazines, including being named the number one resort in Canada and the number one ski resort in North America.

Winter amenities include slope-side access for downhill skiing and snowboarding, snowmobiling, Nordic and heli-skiing, skating and snowshoeing. In summer, guests may enjoy golfing at four designer golf courses, mountain biking, hiking, swimming, fishing, tennis, sightseeing and other activities. The hotel houses a world-class convention centre, state-of-the-art health club and full-service spa.

The hotel's two restaurants, under the direction of executive chef Glenn Monk, offer guests international cuisine highlighted by fresh local Pacific Northwest ingredients. The Wildflower Restaurant specializes in serving nutritious and flavourful breakfasts, daily lunch and dinner. Weekends at The Wildflower feature dinner buffets and a Sunday brunch. The casual Portobello Restaurant operates in a unique market-style atmosphere; diners stroll through pizza, salad, grill, deli, pasta and seafood stations, picking and choosing their fare.

4599 Chateau Boulevard
Whistler, BC   VON 1B0
Telephone: (604) 938-8000;   reservations 1-800-606-8244
Fax: (604) 938-2291
Web site: www.cphotels.ca

Open year-round • Breakfast, lunch and dinner daily
Manager: David Roberts • Executive Chef: Glenn Monk